William Shakespeare (bapt. 26 April 1564 – 23 April 1616) was an English poet, playwright and actor, widely regarded as the greatest writer in the English language and the world's greatest dramatist. He is often called England's national poet and the "Bard of Avon". His extant works, including collaborations, consist of approximately 39 plays, 154 sonnets, two long narrative poems, and a few other verses, some of uncertain authorship. His plays have been translated into every major living language and are performed more often than those of any other playwright. Shakespeare was born and raised in Stratford-upon-Avon, Warwickshire. At the age of 18, he married Anne Hathaway, with whom he had three children: Susanna and twins Hamnet and Judith. Sometime between 1585 and 1592, he began a successful career in London as an actor, writer, and part-owner of a playing company called the Lord Chamberlain's Men, later known as the King's Men. At age 49 (around 1613), he appears to have retired to Stratford, where he died three years later. (Source: Wikipedia)

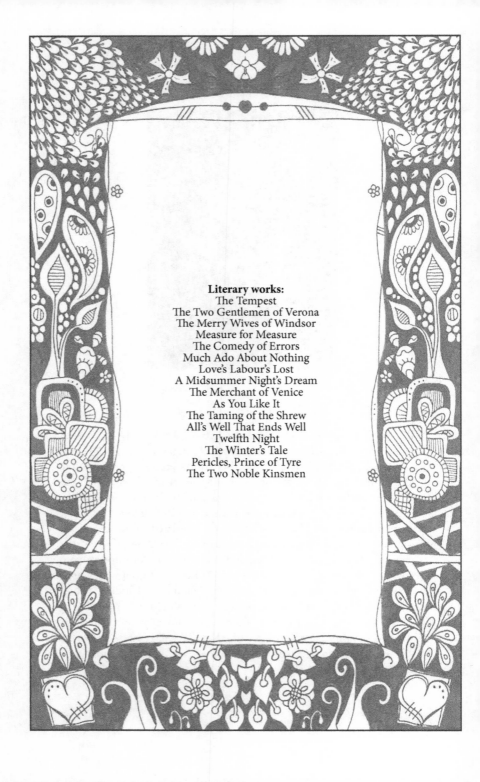

Literary works:
The Tempest
The Two Gentlemen of Verona
The Merry Wives of Windsor
Measure for Measure
The Comedy of Errors
Much Ado About Nothing
Love's Labour's Lost
A Midsummer Night's Dream
The Merchant of Venice
As You Like It
The Taming of the Shrew
All's Well That Ends Well
Twelfth Night
The Winter's Tale
Pericles, Prince of Tyre
The Two Noble Kinsmen

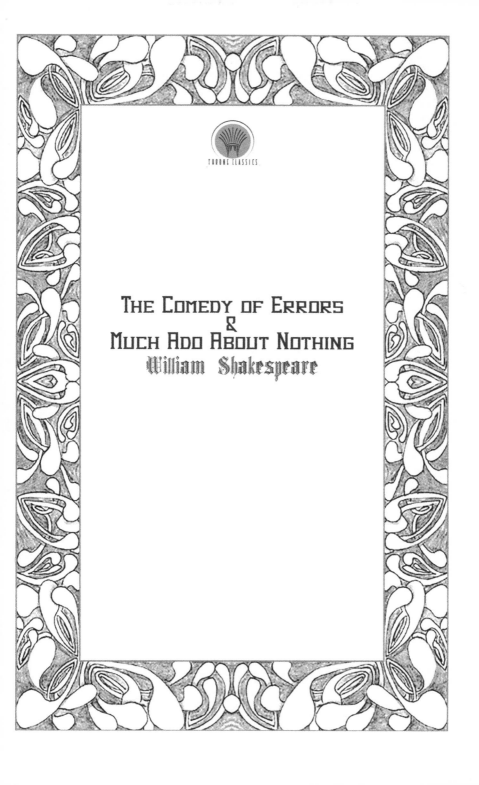

THRONE CLASSICS

THE COMEDY OF ERRORS
&
MUCH ADO ABOUT NOTHING
William Shakespeare

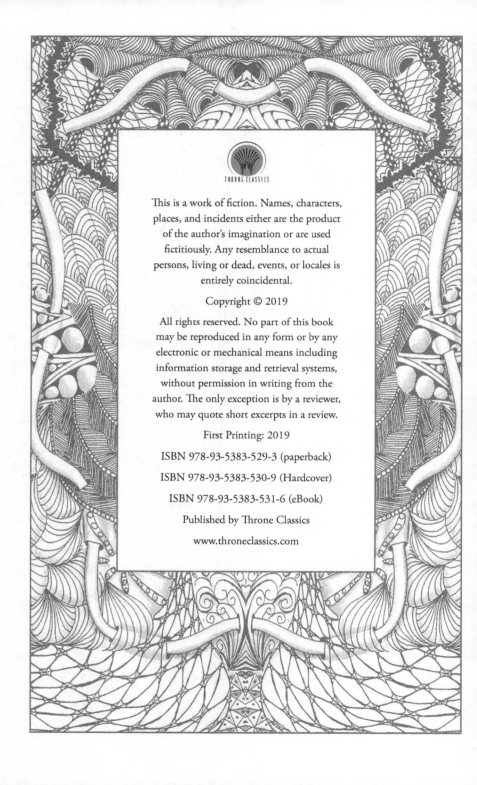

THRONE CLASSICS

Copyright © 2019

First Printing: 2019

ISBN 978-93-5383-529-3 (paperback)

ISBN 978-93-5383-530-9 (Hardcover)

ISBN 978-93-5383-531-6 (eBook)

Published by Throne Classics

www.throneclassics.com

Contents

The Comedy of Errors
&
Much Ado About Nothing

THE COMEDY OF ERRORS

PERSONS REPRESENTED.

SOLINUS, Duke of Ephesus.

AEGEON, a Merchant of Syracuse.

ANTIPHOLUS OF EPHESUS, Twin brothers and sons to Aegion and

ANTIPHOLUS OF SYRACUSE, and Aemelia, but unknown to each other.

DROMIO OF EPHESUS, Twin brothers, and attendants on

DROMIO OF SYRACUSE, the two Antipholuses.

BALTHAZAR, a Merchant.

ANGELO, a Goldsmith.

A MERCHANT, friend to Antipholus of Syracuse.

PINCH, a Schoolmaster and a Conjurer.

AEMILIA, Wife to Aegeon, an Abbess at Ephesus.

ADRIANA, Wife to Antipholus of Ephesus.

LUCIANA, her Sister.

LUCE, her Servant.

A COURTEZAN

Gaoler, Officers, Attendants

SCENE: Ephesus

ACT I.

SCENE 1. A hall in the DUKE'S palace.

[Enter the DUKE, AEGEON, GAOLER, OFFICERS, and other ATTENDANTS.]

AEGEON.

Proceed, Solinus, to procure my fall,

And, by the doom of death, end woes and all.

DUKE.

Merchant of Syracuse, plead no more;

I am not partial to infringe our laws:

The enmity and discord which of late

Sprung from the rancorous outrage of your duke

To merchants, our well-dealing countrymen,—

Who, wanting guilders to redeem their lives,

Have seal'd his rigorous statutes with their bloods,—

Excludes all pity from our threat'ning looks.

For, since the mortal and intestine jars

'Twixt thy seditious countrymen and us,

It hath in solemn synods been decreed,

Both by the Syracusians and ourselves,

To admit no traffic to our adverse towns;

Nay, more,

If any born at Ephesus be seen

At any Syracusian marts and fairs;—

Again, if any Syracusian born

Come to the bay of Ephesus, he dies,

His goods confiscate to the Duke's dispose;

Unless a thousand marks be levied,

To quit the penalty and to ransom him.—

Thy substance, valued at the highest rate,

Cannot amount unto a hundred marks:

Therefore by law thou art condemn'd to die.

AEGEON.

Yet this my comfort,—when your words are done,

My woes end likewise with the evening sun.

DUKE.

Well, Syracusan, say, in brief, the cause

Why thou departedst from thy native home,

And for what cause thou cam'st to Ephesus.

AEGEON.

A heavier task could not have been impos'd

Than I to speak my griefs unspeakable!

Yet, that the world may witness that my end

Was wrought by nature, not by vile offence,

I'll utter what my sorrow gives me leave.

In Syracuse was I born; and wed

Unto a woman, happy but for me,

And by me too, had not our hap been bad.

With her I liv'd in joy; our wealth increas'd

By prosperous voyages I often made

To Epidamnum, till my factor's death,

And he,—great care of goods at random left,—

Drew me from kind embracements of my spouse:

From whom my absence was not six months old,

Before herself,—almost at fainting under

The pleasing punishment that women bear,—

Had made provision for her following me,

And soon and safe arrived where I was.

There had she not been long but she became

A joyful mother of two goodly sons;

And, which was strange, the one so like the other

As could not be disdnguish'd but by names.

That very hour, and in the self-same inn,

A mean woman was delivered

Of such a burden, male twins, both alike:

Those,—for their parents were exceeding poor,—

I bought, and brought up to attend my sons.

My wife, not meanly proud of two such boys,

Made daily motions for our home return:

Unwilling I agreed; alas! too soon!

We came aboard:

A league from Epidamnum had we sail'd

Before the always-wind-obeying deep

Gave any tragic instance of our harm;

But longer did we not retain much hope:

For what obscured light the heavens did grant

Did but convey unto our fearful minds

A doubtful warrant of immediate death;

Which though myself would gladly have embrac'd,

Yet the incessant weepings of my wife,

Weeping before for what she saw must come,

And piteous plainings of the pretty babes,

That mourn'd for fashion, ignorant what to fear,

Forc'd me to seek delays for them and me.

And this it was,—for other means was none.—

The sailors sought for safety by our boat,

And left the ship, then sinking-ripe, to us;:

My wife, more careful for the latter-born,

Had fast'ned him unto a small spare mast,

Such as sea-faring men provide for storms:

To him one of the other twins was bound,

Whilst I had been like heedful of the other.

The children thus dispos'd, my wife and I,

Fixing our eyes on whom our care was fix'd,

Fast'ned ourselves at either end the mast,

And, floating straight, obedient to the stream,

Were carried towards Corinth, as we thought.

At length the sun, gazing upon the earth,

Dispers'd those vapours that offended us;

And, by the benefit of his wish'd light,

The seas wax'd calm, and we discover'd

Two ships from far making amain to us,—

Of Corinth that, of Epidaurus this:

But ere they came—O, let me say no more!—

Gather the sequel by that went before.

DUKE.

Nay, forward, old man, do not break off so;

For we may pity, though not pardon thee.

AEGEON.

O, had the gods done so, I had not now

Worthily term'd them merciless to us!

For, ere the ships could meet by twice five leagues,

We were encount'red by a mighty rock,

Which being violently borne upon,

Our helpful ship was splitted in the midst;

So that, in this unjust divorce of us,

Fortune had left to both of us alike

What to delight in, what to sorrow for.

Her part, poor soul! seeming as burdened

With lesser weight, but not with lesser woe,

Was carried with more speed before the wind;

And in our sight they three were taken up

By fishermen of Corinth, as we thought.

At length another ship had seiz'd on us;

And, knowing whom it was their hap to save,

Gave healthful welcome to their ship-wreck'd guests;

And would have reft the fishers of their prey,

Had not their bark been very slow of sail,

And therefore homeward did they bend their course.—

Thus have you heard me sever'd from my bliss;

That by misfortunes was my life prolong'd,

To tell sad stories of my own mishaps.

DUKE.

And, for the sake of them thou sorrowest for,

Do me the favour to dilate at full

What have befall'n of them and thee till now.

AEGEON.

My youngest boy, and yet my eldest care,

At eighteen years became inquisitive

After his brother, and importun'd me

That his attendant,—so his case was like,

Reft of his brother, but retain'd his name,—

Might bear him company in the quest of him:

Whom whilst I laboured of a love to see,

I hazarded the loss of whom I lov'd.

Five summers have I spent in furthest Greece,

Roaming clean through the bounds of Asia,

And, coasting homeward, came to Ephesus;

Hopeless to find, yet loath to leave unsought

Or that or any place that harbours men.

But here must end the story of my life;

And happy were I in my timely death,

Could all my travels warrant me they live.

DUKE.

Hapless Aegeon, whom the fates have mark'd

To bear the extremity of dire mishap!

Now, trust me, were it not against our laws,

Against my crown, my oath, my dignity,

Which princes, would they, may not disannul,

My soul should sue as advocate for thee.

But though thou art adjudged to the death,

And passed sentence may not be recall'd

But to our honour's great disparagement,

Yet will I favour thee in what I can:

Therefore, merchant, I'll limit thee this day

To seek thy help by beneficial help:

Try all the friends thou hast in Ephesus:

Beg thou, or borrow, to make up the sum,

And live; if not, then thou art doom'd to die.—

Gaoler, take him to thy custody.

GAOLER.

I will, my lord.

AEGEON.

Hopeless and helpless doth Aegeon wend.

But to procrastinate his lifeless end.

[Exeunt.]

SCENE 2. A public place.

[Enter ANTIPHOLUS and DROMIO OF SYRACUSE, and a MERCHANT.]

MERCHANT.

Therefore, give out you are of Epidamnum,

Lest that your goods too soon be confiscate.

This very day a Syracusian merchant

Is apprehended for arrival here;

And, not being able to buy out his life,

According to the statute of the town,

Dies ere the weary sun set in the west.—

There is your money that I had to keep.

ANTIPHOLUS OF SYRACUSE.

Go bear it to the Centaur, where we host,

And stay there, Dromio, till I come to thee.

Within this hour it will be dinner-time;

Till that, I'll view the manners of the town,

Peruse the traders, gaze upon the buildings,

And then return and sleep within mine inn;

For with long travel I am stiff and weary.—

Get thee away.

DROMIO OF SYRACUSE.

Many a man would take you at your word,

And go indeed, having so good a mean.

[Exit DROMIO.]

ANTIPHOLUS OF SYRACUSE.

A trusty villain, sir, that very oft,

When I am dull with care and melancholy,

Lightens my humour with his merry jests.

What, will you walk with me about the town,

And then go to my inn and dine with me?

MERCHANT.

I am invited, sir, to certain merchants,

Of whom I hope to make much benefit:

I crave your pardon. Soon, at five o'clock,

Please you, I'll meet with you upon the mart,

And afterward consort you till bed-time:

My present business calls me from you now.

ANTIPHOLUS OF SYRACUSE.

Farewell till then: I will go lose myself,

And wander up and down to view the city.

MERCHANT.

Sir, I commend you to your own content.

[Exit MERCHANT.]

ANTIPHOLUS OF SYRACUSE.

He that commends me to mine own content

Commends me to the thing I cannot get.

I to the world am like a drop of water

That in the ocean seeks another drop;

Who, failing there to find his fellow forth,

Unseen, inquisitive, confounds himself:

So I, to find a mother and a brother,

In quest of them, unhappy, lose myself.

[Enter DROMIO OF EPHESUS.]

Here comes the almanac of my true date.

What now? How chance thou art return'd so soon?

DROMIO OF EPHESUS.

Return'd so soon! rather approach'd too late.

The capon burns, the pig falls from the spit;

The clock hath strucken twelve upon the bell—

My mistress made it one upon my cheek:

She is so hot because the meat is cold;

The meat is cold because you come not home,;

You come not home because you have no stomach;

You have no stomach, having broke your fast;

But we, that know what 'tis to fast and pray,

Are penitent for your default to-day.

ANTIPHOLUS OF SYRACUSE.

Stop—in your wind, sir; tell me this, I pray:

23

Where have you left the money that I gave you?

DROMIO OF EPHESUS.

O,—sixpence that I had o'Wednesday last

To pay the saddler for my mistress' crupper;—

The saddler had it, sir, I kept it not.

ANTIPHOLUS OF SYRACUSE.

I am not in a sportive humour now;

Tell me, and dally not, where is the money?

We being strangers here, how dar'st thou trust

So great a charge from thine own custody?

DROMIO OF EPHESUS.

I pray you jest, sir, as you sit at dinner:

I from my mistress come to you in post:

If I return, I shall be post indeed;

For she will score your fault upon my pate.

Methinks your maw, like mine, should be your clock,

And strike you home without a messenger.

ANTIPHOLUS OF SYRACUSE.

Come, Dromio, come, these jests are out of season;

Reserve them till a merrier hour than this.

Where is the gold I gave in charge to thee?

DROMIO OF EPHESUS.

To me, sir? why, you gave no gold to me!

ANTIPHOLUS OF SYRACUSE.

Come on, sir knave, have done your foolishness,

And tell me how thou hast dispos'd thy charge.

DROMIO OF EPHESUS.

My charge was but to fetch you from the mart

Home to your house, the Phoenix, sir, to dinner:

My mistress and her sister stay for you.

ANTIPHOLUS OF SYRACUSE.

Now, as I am a Christian, answer me,

In what safe place you have bestow'd my money:

Or I shall break that merry sconce of yours,

That stands on tricks when I am undispos'd;

Where is the thousand marks thou hadst of me?

DROMIO OF EPHESUS.

I have some marks of yours upon my pate,

Some of my mistress' marks upon my shoulders,

But not a thousand marks between you both.—

If I should pay your worship those again,

Perchance you will not bear them patiently.

ANTIPHOLUS OF SYRACUSE.

Thy mistress' marks! what mistress, slave, hast thou?

DROMIO OF EPHESUS.

Your worship's wife, my mistress at the Phoenix;

She that doth fast till you come home to dinner,

And prays that you will hie you home to dinner.

ANTIPHOLUS OF SYRACUSE.

What, wilt thou flout me thus unto my face,

Being forbid? There, take you that, sir knave.

DROMIO OF EPHESUS.

What mean you, sir? for God's sake hold your hands!

Nay, an you will not, sir, I'll take my heels.

[Exit DROMIO.]

ANTIPHOLUS OF SYRACUSE.

Upon my life, by some device or other,

The villain is o'er-raught of all my money.

They say this town is full of cozenage;

As, nimble jugglers that deceive the eye,

Dark-working sorcerers that change the mind,

Soul-killing witches that deform the body,

Disguised cheaters, prating mountebanks,

And many such-like liberties of sin:

If it prove so, I will be gone the sooner.

I'll to the Centaur to go seek this slave:

I greatly fear my money is not safe.

[Exit.]

ACT II.

SCENE 1. A public place.

[Enter ADRIANA and LUCIANA.]

ADRIANA.

Neither my husband nor the slave return'd

That in such haste I sent to seek his master!

Sure, Luciana, it is two o'clock.

LUCIANA.

Perhaps some merchant hath invited him,

And from the mart he's somewhere gone to dinner.

Good sister, let us dine, and never fret:

A man is master of his liberty;

Time is their master; and when they see time,

They'll go or come. If so, be patient, sister.

ADRIANA.

Why should their liberty than ours be more?

LUCIANA.

Because their business still lies out o' door.

ADRIANA.

Look when I serve him so, he takes it ill.

LUCIANA.

O, know he is the bridle of your will.

ADRIANA.

There's none but asses will be bridled so.

LUCIANA.

Why, headstrong liberty is lash'd with woe.

There's nothing situate under heaven's eye

But hath his bound in earth, in sea, in sky;

The beasts, the fishes, and the winged fowls,

Are their males' subjects, and at their controls:

Man, more divine, the masters of all these,

Lord of the wide world and wild wat'ry seas,

Indued with intellectual sense and souls

Of more pre-eminence than fish and fowls,

Are masters to their females, and their lords:

Then let your will attend on their accords.

ADRIANA.

This servitude makes you to keep unwed.

LUCIANA.

Not this, but troubles of the marriage-bed.

ADRIANA.

But, were you wedded, you would bear some sway.

LUCIANA.

Ere I learn love, I'll practise to obey.

ADRIANA.

How if your husband start some other where?

LUCIANA.

Till he come home again, I would forbear.

ADRIANA.

Patience unmov'd, no marvel though she pause:

They can be meek that have no other cause.

A wretched soul, bruis'd with adversity,

We bid be quiet when we hear it cry;

But were we burd'ned with like weight of pain,

As much, or more, we should ourselves complain:

So thou, that hast no unkind mate to grieve thee,

With urging helpless patience would relieve me:

But if thou live to see like right bereft,

This fool-begg'd patience in thee will be left.

LUCIANA.

Well, I will marry one day, but to try:—

Here comes your man, now is your husband nigh.

[Enter DROMIO OF EPHESUS.]

ADRIANA.

Say, is your tardy master now at hand?

DROMIO OF EPHESUS.

Nay, he's at two hands with me, and that my two ears can witness.

ADRIANA.

Say, didst thou speak with him? know'st thou his mind?

DROMIO OF EPHESUS. Ay, ay, he told his mind upon mine ear. Beshrew his hand, I scarce could understand it.

LUCIANA.

Spake he so doubtfully thou could'st not feel his meaning?

DROMIO OF EPHESUS. Nay, he struck so plainly I could too well feel his blows; and withal so doubtfully that I could scarce understand them.

ADRIANA.

But say, I pr'ythee, is he coming home?

It seems he hath great care to please his wife.

DROMIO OF EPHESUS.

Why, mistress, sure my master is horn-mad.

ADRIANA.

Horn-mad, thou villain?

DROMIO OF EPHESUS.

I mean not cuckold-mad; but, sure, he's stark mad.

When I desir'd him to come home to dinner,

He ask'd me for a thousand marks in gold:

"Tis dinner time' quoth I; 'My gold,' quoth he:

'Your meat doth burn' quoth I; 'My gold,' quoth he:

'Will you come home?' quoth I; 'My gold,' quoth he:

'Where is the thousand marks I gave thee, villain?'

'The pig' quoth I 'is burn'd'; 'My gold,' quoth he:

'My mistress, sir,' quoth I; 'Hang up thy mistress;

I know not thy mistress; out on thy mistress!'

LUCIANA.

Quoth who?

DROMIO OF EPHESUS.

Quoth my master:

'I know' quoth he 'no house, no wife, no mistress:'

So that my errand, due unto my tongue,

I thank him, I bare home upon my shoulders;

For, in conclusion, he did beat me there.

ADRIANA.

Go back again, thou slave, and fetch him home.

DROMIO OF EPHESUS.

Go back again! and be new beaten home?

For God's sake, send some other messenger.

ADRIANA.

Back, slave, or I will break thy pate across.

DROMIO OF EPHESUS.

And he will bless that cross with other beating:

Between you I shall have a holy head.

ADRIANA.

Hence, prating peasant: fch thy master home.

DROMIO OF EPHESUS.

Am I so round with you, as you with me,

That like a football you do spurn me thus?

You spurn me hence, and he will spurn me hither:

If I last in this service, you must case me in leather.

[Exit.]

LUCIANA.

Fie, how impatience low'reth in your face!

ADRIANA.

His company must do his minions grace,

Whilst I at home starve for a merry look.

Hath homely age the alluring beauty took

From my poor cheek? then he hath wasted it:

Are my discourses dull? barren my wit?

If voluble and sharp discourse be marr'd,

Unkindness blunts it more than marble hard:

Do their gay vestments his affections bait?

That's not my fault; he's master of my state:

What ruins are in me that can be found

By him not ruin'd? then is he the ground

Of my defeatures: my decayed fair

A sunny look of his would soon repair;

But, too unruly deer, he breaks the pale

And feeds from home; poor I am but his stale.

LUCIANA.

Self-harming jealousy!—fie, beat it hence.

ADRIANA.

Unfeeling fools can with such wrongs dispense.

I know his eye doth homage otherwhere;

Or else what lets it but he would be here?

Sister, you know he promis'd me a chain;—

Would that alone, alone he would detain,

So he would keep fair quarter with his bed!

I see the jewel best enamelled

Will lose his beauty; yet the gold 'bides still

That others touch, yet often touching will

Wear gold; and no man that hath a name

By falsehood and corruption doth it shame.

Since that my beauty cannot please his eye,

I'll weep what's left away, and weeping die.

LUCIANA.

How many fond fools serve mad jealousy!

[Exeunt.]

SCENE 2. The same.

[Enter ANTIPHOLUS OF SYRACUSE.]

ANTIPHOLUS OF SYRACUSE.

The gold I gave to Dromio is laid up

Safe at the Centaur; and the heedful slave

Is wander'd forth in care to seek me out.

By computation and mine host's report

I could not speak with Dromio since at first

I sent him from the mart. See, here he comes.

[Enter DROMIO OF SYRACUSE.]

How now, sir! is your merry humour alter'd?

As you love strokes, so jest with me again.

You know no Centaur? you receiv'd no gold?

Your mistress sent to have me home to dinner?

My house was at the Phoenix? Wast thou mad,

That thus so madly thou didst answer me?

DROMIO OF SYRACUSE.

What answer, sir? when spake I such a word?

ANTIPHOLUS OF SYRACUSE.

Even now, even here, not half-an-hour since.

DROMIO OF SYRACUSE.

I did not see you since you sent me hence,

Home to the Centaur with the gold you gave me.

ANTIPHOLUS OF SYRACUSE.

Villain, thou didst deny the gold's receipt;

And told'st me of a mistress and a dinner;

For which, I hope, thou felt'st I was displeas'd.

DROMIO OF SYRACUSE.

I am glad to see you in this merry vein:

What means this jest? I pray you, master, tell me.

ANTIPHOLUS OF SYRACUSE.

Yea, dost thou jeer and flout me in the teeth?

Think'st thou I jest? Hold, take thou that, and that.

[Beating him.]

DROMIO OF SYRACUSE.

Hold, sir, for God's sake: now your jest is earnest:

Upon what bargain do you give it me?

ANTIPHOLUS OF SYRACUSE.

Because that I familiarly sometimes

Do use you for my fool, and chat with you,

Your sauciness will jest upon my love,

And make a common of my serious hours.

When the sun shines let foolish gnats make sport,

But creep in crannies when he hides his beams.

If you will jest with me, know my aspect,

And fashion your demeanour to my looks,

Or I will beat this method in your sconce.

DROMIO OF SYRACUSE. Sconce, call you it? so you would leave battering, I had rather have it a head: an you use these blows long, I must get a sconce for my head, and ensconce it too; or else I shall seek my wit in my shoulders.—But I pray, sir, why am I beaten?

ANTIPHOLUS OF SYRACUSE.

Dost thou not know?

DROMIO OF SYRACUSE.

Nothing, sir, but that I am beaten.

ANTIPHOLUS OF SYRACUSE.

Shall I tell you why?

DROMIO OF SYRACUSE. Ay, sir, and wherefore; for, they say, every why hath a wherefore.—

ANTIPHOLUS OF SYRACUSE.

Why, first,—for flouting me; and then wherefore,

For urging it the second time to me.

DROMIO OF SYRACUSE.

Was there ever any man thus beaten out of season,

When in the why and the wherefore is neither rhyme nor reason?—

Well, sir, I thank you.

ANTIPHOLUS OF SYRACUSE.

Thank me, sir! for what?

DROMIO OF SYRACUSE.

Marry, sir, for this something that you gave me for nothing.

ANTIPHOLUS OF SYRACUSE.

I'll make you amends next, to give you nothing for something.—

But say, sir, is it dinner-time?

DROMIO OF SYRACUSE.

No, sir; I think the meat wants that I have.

ANTIPHOLUS OF SYRACUSE.

In good time, sir, what's that?

DROMIO OF SYRACUSE.

Basting.

ANTIPHOLUS OF SYRACUSE.

Well, sir, then 'twill be dry.

DROMIO OF SYRACUSE.

If it be, sir, I pray you eat none of it.

ANTIPHOLUS OF SYRACUSE.

Your reason?

DROMIO OF SYRACUSE.

Lest it make you choleric, and purchase me another dry basting.

ANTIPHOLUS OF SYRACUSE.

Well, sir, learn to jest in good time:

There's a time for all things.

DROMIO OF SYRACUSE.

I durst have denied that before you were so choleric.

ANTIPHOLUS OF SYRACUSE.

By what rule, sir?

DROMIO OF SYRACUSE.

Marry, sir, by a rule as plain as the plain bald pate of Father

Time himself.

ANTIPHOLUS OF SYRACUSE.

Let's hear it.

DROMIO OF SYRACUSE. There's no time for a man to recover his hair, that grows bald by nature.

ANTIPHOLUS OF SYRACUSE.

May he not do it by fine and recovery?

DROMIO OF SYRACUSE. Yes, to pay a fine for a peruke, and recover the lost hair of another man.

ANTIPHOLUS OF SYRACUSE. Why is Time such a niggard of hair, being, as it is, so plentiful an excrement?

DROMIO OF SYRACUSE. Because it is a blessing that he bestows on beasts: and what he hath scanted men in hair he hath given them in wit.

ANTIPHOLUS OF SYRACUSE.

Why, but there's many a man hath more hair than wit.

DROMIO OF SYRACUSE.

Not a man of those but he hath the wit to lose his hair.

ANTIPHOLUS OF SYRACUSE.

Why, thou didst conclude hairy men plain dealers without wit.

DROMIO OF SYRACUSE. The plainer dealer, the sooner lost: yet he loseth it in a kind of jollity.

ANTIPHOLUS OF SYRACUSE.

For what reason?

DROMIO OF SYRACUSE.

For two; and sound ones too.

ANTIPHOLUS OF SYRACUSE.

Nay, not sound, I pray you.

DROMIO OF SYRACUSE.

Sure ones, then.

ANTIPHOLUS OF SYRACUSE.

Nay, not sure, in a thing falsing.

DROMIO OF SYRACUSE.

Certain ones, then.

ANTIPHOLUS OF SYRACUSE.

Name them.

DROMIO OF SYRACUSE. The one, to save the money that he spends in tiring; the other, that at dinner they should not drop in his porridge.

ANTIPHOLUS OF SYRACUSE. You would all this time have proved there is no time for all things.

DROMIO OF SYRACUSE. Marry, and did, sir; namely, no time to recover hair lost by nature.

ANTIPHOLUS OF SYRACUSE. But your reason was not substantial why there is no time to recover.

DROMIO OF SYRACUSE. Thus I mend it: Time himself is bald, and, therefore, to the world's end will have bald followers.

ANTIPHOLUS OF SYRACUSE.

I knew 't'would be a bald conclusion:

But, soft! who wafts us yonder?

[Enter ADRIANA and LUCIANA.]

ADRIANA.

Ay, ay, Antipholus, look strange and frown;

Some other mistress hath thy sweet aspects:

I am not Adriana, nor thy wife.

The time was, once, when thou unurg'd wouldst vow

That never words were music to thine ear,

That never object pleasing in thine eye,

That never touch well welcome to thy hand,

That never meat sweet-savour'd in thy taste,

Unless I spake, or look'd, or touch'd, or carv'd to thee.

How comes it now, my husband, oh, how comes it,

That thou art then estranged from thyself?

Thyself I call it, being strange to me,

That, undividable, incorporate,

Am better than thy dear self's better part.

Ah, do not tear away thyself from me;

For know, my love, as easy mayst thou fall

A drop of water in the breaking gulf,

And take unmingled thence that drop again,

Without addition or diminishing,

As take from me thyself, and not me too.

How dearly would it touch thee to the quick,

Should'st thou but hear I were licentious,

And that this body, consecrate to thee,

By ruffian lust should be contaminate!

Wouldst thou not spit at me and spurn at me,

And hurl the name of husband in my face,

And tear the stain'd skin off my harlot brow,

And from my false hand cut the wedding-ring,

And break it with a deep-divorcing vow?

I know thou canst; and, therefore, see thou do it.

I am possess'd with an adulterate blot;

My blood is mingled with the crime of lust:

For if we two be one, and thou play false,

I do digest the poison of thy flesh,

Being strumpeted by thy contagion.

Keep then fair league and truce with thy true bed;

I live dis-stain'd, thou undishonoured.

ANTIPHOLUS OF SYRACUSE.

Plead you to me, fair dame? I know you not:

In Ephesus I am but two hours old,

As strange unto your town as to your talk;

Who, every word by all my wit being scann'd,

Want wit in all one word to understand.

LUCIANA.

Fie, brother! how the world is chang'd with you:

When were you wont to use my sister thus?

She sent for you by Dromio home to dinner.

ANTIPHOLUS OF SYRACUSE.

By Dromio?

DROMIO OF SYRACUSE.

By me?

ADRIANA.

By thee; and this thou didst return from him,—

That he did buffet thee, and in his blows

Denied my house for his, me for his wife.

ANTIPHOLUS OF SYRACUSE.

Did you converse, sir, with this gentlewoman?

What is the course and drift of your compact?

DROMIO OF SYRACUSE.

I, sir? I never saw her till this time.

ANTIPHOLUS OF SYRACUSE.

Villain, thou liest; for even her very words

Didst thou deliver to me on the mart.

DROMIO OF SYRACUSE.

I never spake with her in all my life.

ANTIPHOLUS OF SYRACUSE.

How can she thus, then, call us by our names,

Unless it be by inspiration?

ADRIANA.

How ill agrees it with your gravity

To counterfeit thus grossly with your slave,

Abetting him to thwart me in my mood!

Be it my wrong, you are from me exempt,

But wrong not that wrong with a more contempt.

Come, I will fasten on this sleeve of thine:

Thou art an elm, my husband, I a vine,

Whose weakness, married to thy stronger state,

Makes me with thy strength to communicate:

If aught possess thee from me, it is dross,

Usurping ivy, brier, or idle moss;

Who all, for want of pruning, with intrusion

Infect thy sap, and live on thy confusion.

ANTIPHOLUS OF SYRACUSE.

To me she speaks; she moves me for her theme:

What, was I married to her in my dream?

Or sleep I now, and think I hear all this?

What error drives our eyes and ears amiss?

Until I know this sure uncertainty

I'll entertain the offer'd fallacy.

LUCIANA.

Dromio, go bid the servants spread for dinner.

DROMIO OF SYRACUSE.

O, for my beads! I cross me for a sinner.

This is the fairy land;—O spite of spites!

We talk with goblins, owls, and sprites;

If we obey them not, this will ensue,

They'll suck our breath, or pinch us black and blue.

LUCIANA.

Why prat'st thou to thyself, and answer'st not?

Dromio, thou drone, thou snail, thou slug, thou sot!

DROMIO OF SYRACUSE.

I am transformed, master, am not I?

ANTIPHOLUS OF SYRACUSE.

I think thou art in mind, and so am I.

DROMIO OF SYRACUSE.

Nay, master, both in mind and in my shape.

ANTIPHOLUS OF SYRACUSE.

Thou hast thine own form.

DROMIO OF SYRACUSE.

No, I am an ape.

LUCIANA.

If thou art chang'd to aught, 'tis to an ass.

DROMIO OF SYRACUSE.

'Tis true; she rides me, and I long for grass.

'Tis so, I am an ass; else it could never be

But I should know her as well as she knows me.

ADRIANA.

Come, come, no longer will I be a fool,

To put the finger in the eye and weep,

Whilst man and master laughs my woes to scorn.—

Come, sir, to dinner;—Dromio, keep the gate:—

Husband, I'll dine above with you to-day,

And shrive you of a thousand idle pranks:—

Sirrah, if any ask you for your master,

Say he dines forth, and let no creature enter.—

Come, sister:—Dromio, play the porter well.

ANTIPHOLUS OF SYRACUSE.

Am I in earth, in heaven, or in hell?

Sleeping or waking, mad, or well-advis'd?

Known unto these, and to myself disguis'd!

I'll say as they say, and persever so,

And in this mist at all adventures go.

DROMIO OF SYRACUSE.

Master, shall I be porter at the gate?

ADRIANA.

Ay; and let none enter, lest I break your pate.

LUCIANA.

Come, come, Antipholus, we dine too late.

[Exeunt.]

ACT III.

SCENE 1. The same.

[Enter ANTIPHOLUS OF EPHESUS, DROMIO OF EPHESUS, ANGELO, and BALTHAZAR.]

ANTIPHOLUS OF EPHESUS.

Good Signior Angelo, you must excuse us all.

My wife is shrewish when I keep not hours:

Say that I linger'd with you at your shop

To see the making of her carcanet,

And that to-morrow you will bring it home.

But here's a villain that would face me down.

He met me on the mart; and that I beat him,

And charg'd him with a thousand marks in gold;

And that I did deny my wife and house:—

Thou drunkard, thou, what didst thou mean by this?

DROMIO OF EPHESUS.

Say what you will, sir, but I know what I know:

That you beat me at the mart I have your hand to show;

If the skin were parchment, and the blows you gave were ink,

Your own handwriting would tell you what I think.

ANTIPHOLUS OF EPHESUS.

I think thou art an ass.

DROMIO OF EPHESUS.

Marry, so it doth appear

By the wrongs I suffer and the blows I bear.

I should kick, being kick'd; and being at that pass,

You would keep from my heels, and beware of an ass.

ANTIPHOLUS OF EPHESUS.

You are sad, Signior Balthazar; pray God our cheer

May answer my good will and your good welcome here.

BALTHAZAR.

I hold your dainties cheap, sir, and your welcome dear.

ANTIPHOLUS OF EPHESUS.

O, Signior Balthazar, either at flesh or fish,

A table full of welcome makes scarce one dainty dish.

BALTHAZAR.

Good meat, sir, is common; that every churl affords.

ANTIPHOLUS OF EPHESUS.

And welcome more common; for that's nothing but words.

BALTHAZAR

Small cheer and great welcome makes a merry feast.

ANTIPHOLUS OF EPHESUS.

Ay, to a niggardly host and more sparing guest.

But though my cates be mean, take them in good part;

Better cheer may you have, but not with better heart.

But, soft; my door is lock'd: go bid them let us in.

DROMIO OF EPHESUS.

Maud, Bridget, Marian, Cicely, Gillian, Jen!

DROMIO OF SYRACUSE.

[Within] Mome, malt-horse, capon, coxcomb, idiot, patch!

Either get thee from the door, or sit down at the hatch:

Dost thou conjure for wenches, that thou call'st for such store,

When one is one too many? Go, get thee from the door.

DROMIO OF EPHESUS.

What patch is made our porter? My master stays in the street.

DROMIO OF SYRACUSE.

Let him walk from whence he came, lest he catch cold on's feet.

ANTIPHOLUS OF EPHESUS.

Who talks within there? Ho, open the door!

DROMIO OF SYRACUSE.

Right, sir; I'll tell you when an you'll tell me wherefore.

ANTIPHOLUS OF EPHESUS.

Wherefore! For my dinner: I have not dined to-day.

DROMIO OF SYRACUSE.

Nor to-day here you must not; come again when you may.

ANTIPHOLUS OF EPHESUS.

What art thou that keep'st me out from the house I owe?

DROMIO OF SYRACUSE.

The porter for this time, sir, and my name is Dromio.

DROMIO OF EPHESUS.

O villain, thou hast stolen both mine office and my name;

The one ne'er got me credit, the other mickle blame.

If thou hadst been Dromio to-day in my place,

Thou wouldst have chang'd thy face for a name, or thy name for an

ass.

LUCE. [Within.] What a coil is there! Dromio, who are those at the
gate?

DROMIO OF EPHESUS.

Let my master in, Luce.

LUCE.

Faith, no, he comes too late;

And so tell your master.

DROMIO OF EPHESUS.

O Lord, I must laugh;—

Have at you with a proverb:—Shall I set in my staff?

LUCE.

Have at you with another: that's—When? can you tell?

DROMIO OF SYRACUSE.

If thy name be called Luce,—Luce, thou hast answer'd him well.

ANTIPHOLUS OF EPHESUS.

Do you hear, you minion? you'll let us in, I hope?

LUCE.

I thought to have ask'd you.

DROMIO OF SYRACUSE.

And you said no.

DROMIO OF EPHESUS.

So, Come, help: well struck; there was blow for blow.

ANTIPHOLUS OF EPHESUS.

Thou baggage, let me in.

LUCE.

Can you tell for whose sake?

DROMIO OF EPHESUS.

Master, knock the door hard.

LUCE.

Let him knock till it ache.

ANTIPHOLUS OF EPHESUS.

You'll cry for this, minion, if I beat the door down.

LUCE.

What needs all that, and a pair of stocks in the town?

ADRIANA.

[Within.] Who is that at the door, that keeps all this noise?

DROMIO OF SYRACUSE.

By my troth, your town is troubled with unruly boys.

ANTIPHOLUS OF EPHESUS.

Are you there, wife? you might have come before.

ADRIANA.

Your wife, sir knave! go, get you from the door.

DROMIO OF EPHESUS.

If you went in pain, master, this knave would go sore.

ANGELO. Here is neither cheer, sir, nor welcome: we would fain have either.

BALTHAZAR.

In debating which was best, we shall part with neither.

DROMIO OF EPHESUS.

They stand at the door, master; bid them welcome hither.

ANTIPHOLUS OF EPHESUS.

There is something in the wind, that we cannot get in.

DROMIO OF EPHESUS.

You would say so, master, if your garments were thin.

Your cake here is warm within; you stand here in the cold:

It would make a man mad as a buck, to be so bought and sold.

ANTIPHOLUS OF EPHESUS.

Go, fetch me something, I'll break ope the gate.

DROMIO OF SYRACUSE.

Break any breaking here, and I'll break your knave's pate.

DROMIO OF EPHESUS.

A man may break a word with you, sir; and words are but wind;

Ay, and break it in your face, so he break it not behind.

DROMIO OF SYRACUSE.

It seems thou want'st breaking; out upon thee, hind!

DROMIO OF EPHESUS.

Here's too much out upon thee: I pray thee, let me in.

DROMIO OF SYRACUSE.

Ay, when fowls have no feathers and fish have no fin.

ANTIPHOLUS OF EPHESUS.

Well, I'll break in; go borrow me a crow.

DROMIO OF EPHESUS.

A crow without feather; master, mean you so?

For a fish without a fin, there's a fowl without a feather:

If a crow help us in, sirrah, we'll pluck a crow together.

ANTIPHOLUS OF EPHESUS.

Go, get thee gone; fetch me an iron crow.

BALTHAZAR.

Have patience, sir: O, let it not be so:

Herein you war against your reputation,

And draw within the compass of suspect

The unviolated honour of your wife.

Once this,—your long experience of her wisdom,

Her sober virtue, years, and modesty,

Plead on her part some cause to you unknown;

And doubt not, sir, but she will well excuse

Why at this time the doors are made against you.

Be rul'd by me; depart in patience,

And let us to the Tiger all to dinner:

And, about evening, come yourself alone,

To know the reason of this strange restraint.

If by strong hand you offer to break in,

Now in the stirring passage of the day,

A vulgar comment will be made of it;

And that supposed by the common rout

Against your yet ungalled estimation

That may with foul intrusion enter in,

And dwell upon your grave when you are dead:

For slander lives upon succession,

For ever hous'd where it gets possession.

ANTIPHOLUS OF EPHESUS.

You have prevail'd. I will depart in quiet,

And, in despite of mirth, mean to be merry.

I know a wench of excellent discourse,—

Pretty and witty; wild, and yet, too, gentle;—

There will we dine: this woman that I mean,

My wife,—but, I protest, without desert,—

Hath oftentimes upbraided me withal;

To her will we to dinner.—Get you home

And fetch the chain: by this I know 'tis made:

Bring it, I pray you, to the Porcupine;

For there's the house; that chain will I bestow,—

Be it for nothing but to spite my wife,—-

Upon mine hostess there: good sir, make haste:

Since mine own doors refuse to entertain me,

I'll knock elsewhere, to see if they'll disdain me.

ANGELO.

I'll meet you at that place some hour hence.

ANTIPHOLUS OF EPHESUS.

Do so; this jest shall cost me some expense.

[Exeunt.]

SCENE 2. The same.

[Enter LUCIANA with ANTIPHOLUS OF SYRACUSE.]

LUCIANA.

And may it be that you have quite forgot

  A husband's office? Shall, Antipholus,

Even in the spring of love, thy love-springs rot?

  Shall love, in building, grow so ruinate?

If you did wed my sister for her wealth,

  Then for her wealth's sake use her with more kindness;

Or, if you like elsewhere, do it by stealth;

  Muffle your false love with some show of blindness;

Let not my sister read it in your eye;

  Be not thy tongue thy own shame's orator;

Look sweet, speak fair, become disloyalty;

  Apparel vice like virtue's harbinger;

Bear a fair presence though your heart be tainted;

  Teach sin the carriage of a holy saint;

Be secret-false: what need she be acquainted?

  What simple thief brags of his own attaint?

'Tis double wrong, to truant with your bed

  And let her read it in thy looks at board:—

Shame hath a bastard fame, well managed;

Ill deeds is doubled with an evil word.

Alas, poor women! make us but believe,

  Being compact of credit, that you love us:

Though others have the arm, show us the sleeve;

  We in your motion turn, and you may move us.

Then, gentle brother, get you in again;

  Comfort my sister, cheer her, call her wife:

'Tis holy sport to be a little vain

  When the sweet breath of flattery conquers strife.

ANTIPHOLUS OF SYRACUSE.

Sweet mistress,—what your name is else, I know not,

  Nor by what wonder you do hit on mine,—

Less, in your knowledge and your grace, you show not

  Than our earth's wonder: more than earth divine.

Teach me, dear creature, how to think and speak;

  Lay open to my earthy gross conceit,

Smother'd in errors, feeble, shallow, weak,

  The folded meaning of your words' deceit.

Against my soul's pure truth why labour you

  To make it wander in an unknown field?

Are you a god? would you create me new?

  Transform me, then, and to your power I'll yield.

But if that I am I, then well I know

Your weeping sister is no wife of mine,

Nor to her bed no homage do I owe:

Far more, far more, to you do I decline.

O, train me not, sweet mermaid, with thy note,

To drown me in thy sister's flood of tears:

Sing, siren, for thyself, and I will dote;

Spread o'er the silver waves thy golden hairs,

And as a bed I'll take thee, and there lie;

And, in that glorious supposition, think

He gains by death that hath such means to die:—

Let love, being light, be drowned if she sink!

LUCIANA.

What, are you mad, that you do reason so?

ANTIPHOLUS OF SYRACUSE.

Not mad, but mated; how, I do not know.

LUCIANA.

It is a fault that springeth from your eye.

ANTIPHOLUS OF SYRACUSE.

For gazing on your beams, fair sun, being by.

LUCIANA.

Gaze where you should, and that will clear your sight.

ANTIPHOLUS OF SYRACUSE.

As good to wink, sweet love, as look on night.

LUCIANA.

Why call you me love? call my sister so.

ANTIPHOLUS OF SYRACUSE.

Thy sister's sister.

LUCIANA.

That's my sister.

ANTIPHOLUS OF SYRACUSE.

No;

It is thyself, mine own self's better part;

Mine eye's clear eye, my dear heart's dearer heart;

My food, my fortune, and my sweet hope's aim,

My sole earth's heaven, and my heaven's claim.

LUCIANA.

All this my sister is, or else should be.

ANTIPHOLUS OF SYRACUSE.

Call thyself sister, sweet, for I aim thee;

Thee will I love, and with thee lead my life:

Thou hast no husband yet, nor I no wife;

Give me thy hand.

LUCIANA.

O, soft, sir, hold you still;

I'll fetch my sister to get her good-will.

[Exit LUCIANA.]

[Enter from the house of ANTIPHOLUS OF EPHESUS, DROMIO OF SYRACUSE.]

ANTIPHOLUS OF SYRACUSE.

Why, how now, Dromio? where runn'st thou so fast?

DROMIO OF SYRACUSE.

Do you know me, sir? am I Dromio? am I your man? am I myself?

ANTIPHOLUS OF SYRACUSE.

Thou art Dromio, thou art my man, thou art thyself.

DROMIO OF SYRACUSE.

I am an ass, I am a woman's man, and beside myself.

ANTIPHOLUS OF SYRACUSE.

What woman's man? and how besides thyself?

DROMIO OF SYRACUSE. Marry, sir, besides myself, I am due to a woman; one that claims me, one that haunts me, one that will have me.

ANTIPHOLUS OF SYRACUSE.

What claim lays she to thee?

DROMIO OF SYRACUSE. Marry, sir, such claim as you would lay to your horse: and she would have me as a beast; not that, I being a beast, she would have me; but that she, being a very beastly creature, lays claim to me.

ANTIPHOLUS OF SYRACUSE.

What is she?

DROMIO OF SYRACUSE. A very reverent body; ay, such a one as a man may not speak of without he say sir-reverence. I have but lean luck in the match, and yet is she a wondrous fat marriage.

ANTIPHOLUS OF SYRACUSE.

How dost thou mean?—a fat marriage?

DROMIO OF SYRACUSE. Marry, sir, she's the kitchen-wench, and all grease; and I know not what use to put her to, but to make a lamp of her and run from her by her own light. I warrant, her rags, and the tallow in them will burn a Poland winter: if she lives till doomsday, she'll burn week longer than the whole world.

ANTIPHOLUS OF SYRACUSE.

What complexion is she of?

DROMIO OF SYRACUSE. Swart, like my shoe; but her face nothing like so clean kept: for why? she sweats, a man may go over shoes in the grime of it.

ANTIPHOLUS OF SYRACUSE.

That's a fault that water will mend.

DROMIO OF SYRACUSE.

No, sir, 'tis in grain; Noah's flood could not do it.

ANTIPHOLUS OF SYRACUSE.

What's her name?

DROMIO OF SYRACUSE. Nell, sir; but her name and three-quarters, that is an ell and three quarters, will not measure her from hip to hip.

ANTIPHOLUS OF SYRACUSE.

Then she bears some breadth?

DROMIO OF SYRACUSE. No longer from head to foot than from hip to hip: she is spherical, like a globe: I could find out countries in her.

ANTIPHOLUS OF SYRACUSE.

In what part of her body stands Ireland?

DROMIO OF SYRACUSE.

Marry, sir, in her buttocks; I found it out by the bogs.

ANTIPHOLUS OF SYRACUSE.

Where Scotland?

DROMIO OF SYRACUSE.

I found it by the barrenness, hard in the palm of the hand.

ANTIPHOLUS OF SYRACUSE.

Where France?

DROMIO OF SYRACUSE.

In her forehead; armed and reverted, making war against her hair.

ANTIPHOLUS OF SYRACUSE.

Where England?

DROMIO OF SYRACUSE. I looked for the chalky cliffs, but I could find no whiteness in them; but I guess it stood in her chin, by the salt rheum that ran between France and it.

ANTIPHOLUS OF SYRACUSE.

Where Spain?

DROMIO OF SYRACUSE.

Faith, I saw it not; but I felt it hot in her breath.

ANTIPHOLUS OF SYRACUSE.

Where America,—the Indies?

DROMIO OF SYRACUSE. O, sir, upon her nose, an o'er embellished with rubies, carbuncles, sapphires, declining their rich aspect to the hot breath of Spain; who sent whole armadoes of carracks to be ballast at her nose.

ANTIPHOLUS OF SYRACUSE.

Where stood Belgia,—the Netherlands?

DROMIO OF SYRACUSE. O, sir, I did not look so low.—To conclude: this drudge or diviner laid claim to me; called me Dromio; swore I was assured to her; told me what privy marks I had about me, as the mark of my shoulder, the mole in my neck, the great wart on my left arm, that I, amazed, ran from her as a witch: and, I think, if my breast had not been made of faith and my heart of steel, she had transformed me to a curtail-dog, and made me turn i' the wheel.

ANTIPHOLUS OF SYRACUSE.

Go, hie thee presently post to the road;

An if the wind blow any way from shore,

I will not harbour in this town to-night.

If any bark put forth, come to the mart,

Where I will walk till thou return to me.

If every one knows us, and we know none,

'Tis time, I think, to trudge, pack and be gone.

DROMIO OF SYRACUSE.

As from a bear a man would run for life,

So fly I from her that would be my wife.

[Exit.]

ANTIPHOLUS OF SYRACUSE.

There's none but witches do inhabit here;

And therefore 'tis high time that I were hence.

She that doth call me husband, even my soul

Doth for a wife abhor; but her fair sister,

Possess'd with such a gentle sovereign grace,

Of such enchanting presence and discourse,

Hath almost made me traitor to myself:

But, lest myself be guilty to self-wrong,

I'll stop mine ears against the mermaid's song.

[Enter ANGELO.]

ANGELO.

Master Antipholus?

ANTIPHOLUS OF SYRACUSE.

Ay, that's my name.

ANGELO.

I know it well, sir. Lo, here is the chain;

I thought to have ta'en you at the Porcupine:

The chain unfinish'd made me stay thus long.

ANTIPHOLUS OF SYRACUSE.

What is your will that I shall do with this?

ANGELO.

What please yourself, sir; I have made it for you.

ANTIPHOLUS OF SYRACUSE.

Made it for me, sir! I bespoke it not.

ANGELO.

Not once nor twice, but twenty times you have:

Go home with it, and please your wife withal;

And soon at supper-time I'll visit you,

And then receive my money for the chain.

ANTIPHOLUS OF SYRACUSE.

I pray you, sir, receive the money now,

For fear you ne'er see chain nor money more.

ANGELO.

You are a merry man, sir; fare you well.

[Exit.]

ANTIPHOLUS OF SYRACUSE.

What I should think of this I cannot tell:

But this I think, there's no man is so vain

That would refuse so fair an offer'd chain.

I see a man here needs not live by shifts,

When in the streets he meets such golden gifts.

I'll to the mart, and there for Dromio stay;

If any ship put out, then straight away.

[Exit.]

ACT IV.

SCENE 1. The same.

[Enter a MERCHANT, ANGELO, and an OFFICER.]

MERCHANT.

You know, since Pentecost the sum is due,

And since I have not much importun'd you;

Nor now I had not, but that I am bound

To Persia, and want guilders for my voyage;

Therefore make present satisfaction,

Or I'll attach you by this officer.

ANGELO.

Even just the sum that I do owe to you

Is growing to me by Antipholus;

And in the instant that I met with you

He had of me a chain; at five o'clock

I shall receive the money for the same:

Pleaseth you walk with me down to his house,

I will discharge my bond, and thank you too.

[Enter ANTIPHOLUS OF EPHESUS, and DROMIO OF EPHESUS.]

OFFICER.

That labour may you save: see where he comes.

ANTIPHOLUS OF EPHESUS.

While I go to the goldsmith's house, go thou

And buy a rope's end; that will I bestow

Among my wife and her confederates,

For locking me out of my doors by day.—

But, soft; I see the goldsmith: get thee gone;

Buy thou a rope, and bring it home to me.

DROMIO OF EPHESUS.

I buy a thousand pound a year! I buy a rope!

[Exit DROMIO.]

ANTIPHOLUS OF EPHESUS.

A man is well holp up that trusts to you:

I promised your presence, and the chain;

But neither chain nor goldsmith came to me:

Belike you thought our love would last too long,

If it were chain'd together; and therefore came not.

ANGELO.

Saving your merry humour, here's the note,

How much your chain weighs to the utmost carat;

The fineness of the gold, and chargeful fashion;

Which doth amount to three odd ducats more

Than I stand debted to this gentleman:

I pray you, see him presently discharg'd,

For he is bound to sea, and stays but for it.

ANTIPHOLUS OF EPHESUS.

I am not furnished with the present money;

Besides I have some business in the town:

Good Signior, take the stranger to my house,

And with you take the chain, and bid my wife

Disburse the sum on the receipt thereof;

Perchance I will be there as soon as you.

ANGELO.

Then you will bring the chain to her yourself?

ANTIPHOLUS OF EPHESUS.

No; bear it with you, lest I come not time enough.

ANGELO.

Well, sir, I will: have you the chain about you?

ANTIPHOLUS OF EPHESUS.

An if I have not, sir, I hope you have,

Or else you may return without your money.

ANGELO.

Nay, come, I pray you, sir, give me the chain;

Both wind and tide stays for this gentleman,

And I, to blame, have held him here too long.

ANTIPHOLUS OF EPHESUS.

Good Lord, you use this dalliance to excuse

Your breach of promise to the Porcupine:

I should have chid you for not bringing it,

But, like a shrew, you first begin to brawl.

MERCHANT.

The hour steals on; I pray you, sir, despatch.

ANGELO.

You hear how he importunes me: the chain,—

ANTIPHOLUS OF EPHESUS.

Why, give it to my wife, and fetch your money.

ANGELO.

Come, come, you know I gave it you even now;

Either send the chain or send by me some token.

ANTIPHOLUS OF EPHESUS.

Fie! now you run this humour out of breath:

Come, where's the chain? I pray you, let me see it.

MERCHANT.

My business cannot brook this dalliance:

Good sir, say whe'r you'll answer me or no;

If not, I'll leave him to the officer.

ANTIPHOLUS OF EPHESUS.

I answer you! What should I answer you?

ANGELO.

The money that you owe me for the chain.

ANTIPHOLUS OF EPHESUS.

I owe you none till I receive the chain.

ANGELO.

You know I gave it you half-an-hour since.

ANTIPHOLUS OF EPHESUS.

You gave me none: you wrong me much to say so.

ANGELO.

You wrong me more, sir, in denying it:

Consider how it stands upon my credit.

MERCHANT.

Well, officer, arrest him at my suit.

OFFICER.

I do; and charge you in the duke's name to obey me.

ANGELO.

This touches me in reputation:

Either consent to pay this sum for me,

Or I attach you by this officer.

ANTIPHOLUS OF EPHESUS.

Consent to pay thee that I never had!

Arrest me, foolish fellow, if thou dar'st.

ANGELO.

Here is thy fee; arrest him, officer:—

I would not spare my brother in this case,

If he should scorn me so apparently.

OFFICER.

I do arrest you, sir: you hear the suit.

ANTIPHOLUS OF EPHESUS.

I do obey thee till I give thee bail:—

But, sirrah, you shall buy this sport as dear

As all the metal in your shop will answer.

ANGELO.

Sir, sir, I shall have law in Ephesus,

To your notorious shame, I doubt it not.

[Enter DROMIO OF SYRACUSE.]

DROMIO OF SYRACUSE.

Master, there's a bark of Epidamnum

That stays but till her owner comes aboard,

And then, sir, bears away: our fraughtage, sir,

I have convey'd aboard; and I have bought

The oil, the balsamum, and aqua-vitae.

The ship is in her trim; the merry wind

Blows fair from land; they stay for nought at all

But for their owner, master, and yourself.

ANTIPHOLUS OF EPHESUS.

How now! a madman? Why, thou peevish sheep,

What ship of Epidamnum stays for me?

DROMIO OF SYRACUSE.

A ship you sent me to, to hire waftage.

ANTIPHOLUS OF EPHESUS.

Thou drunken slave! I sent the for a rope;

And told thee to what purpose and what end.

DROMIO OF SYRACUSE.

You sent me, sir, for a rope's end as soon:

You sent me to the bay, sir, for a bark.

ANTIPHOLUS OF EPHESUS.

I will debate this matter at more leisure,

And teach your ears to list me with more heed.

To Adriana, villain, hie thee straight:

Give her this key, and tell her, in the desk

That's cover'd o'er with Turkish tapestry

There is a purse of ducats; let her send it:

Tell her I am arrested in the street,

And that shall bail me: hie thee, slave; be gone.

On, officer, to prison till it come.

[Exeunt MERCHANT, ANGELO, OFFICER, and ANTIPHOLUS
OF EPHESUS.]

DROMIO OF SYRACUSE.

To Adriana! that is where we din'd,

Where Dowsabel did claim me for her husband:

She is too big, I hope, for me to compass.

Thither I must, although against my will,

For servants must their masters' minds fulfil.

[Exit.]

SCENE 2. The same.

[Enter ADRIANA and LUCIANA.]

ADRIANA.

Ah, Luciana, did he tempt thee so?

  Might'st thou perceive austerely in his eye

That he did plead in earnest, yea or no?

  Look'd he or red or pale, or sad or merrily?

What observation mad'st thou in this case

Of his heart's meteors tilting in his face?

LUCIANA.

First he denied you had in him no right.

ADRIANA.

He meant he did me none; the more my spite.

LUCIANA.

Then swore he that he was a stranger here.

ADRIANA.

And true he swore, though yet forsworn he were.

LUCIANA.

Then pleaded I for you.

ADRIANA.

And what said he?

LUCIANA.

That love I begg'd for you he begg'd of me.

ADRIANA.

With what persuasion did he tempt thy love?

LUCIANA.

With words that in an honest suit might move.

First he did praise my beauty, then my speech.

ADRIANA.

Didst speak him fair?

LUCIANA.

Have patience, I beseech.

ADRIANA.

I cannot, nor I will not hold me still;

My tongue, though not my heart, shall have his will.

He is deformed, crooked, old, and sere,

Ill-fac'd, worse bodied, shapeless everywhere;

Vicious, ungentle, foolish, blunt, unkind;

Stigmatical in making, worse in mind.

LUCIANA.

Who would be jealous then of such a one?

No evil lost is wail'd when it is gone.

ADRIANA.

Ah! but I think him better than I say,

And yet would herein others' eyes were worse:

Far from her nest the lapwing cries, away;

My heart prays for him, though my tongue do curse.

[Enter DROMIO OF SYRACUSE.]

DROMIO OF SYRACUSE.

Here, go; the desk, the purse: sweet now, make haste.

LUCIANA.

How hast thou lost thy breath?

DROMIO OF SYRACUSE.

By running fast.

ADRIANA.

Where is thy master, Dromio? is he well?

DROMIO OF SYRACUSE.

No, he's in Tartar limbo, worse than hell.

A devil in an everlasting garment hath him;

One whose hard heart is button'd up with steel;

A fiend, a fairy, pitiless and rough;

A wolf—nay worse, a fellow all in buff;

A back-friend, a shoulder-clapper, one that countermands

The passages of alleys, creeks, and narrow lands;

A hound that runs counter, and yet draws dry foot well;

One that, before the judgment, carries poor souls to hell.

ADRIANA.

Why, man, what is the matter?

DROMIO OF SYRACUSE.

I do not know the matter: he is 'rested on the case.

ADRIANA.

What, is he arrested? tell me at whose suit?

DROMIO OF SYRACUSE.

I know not at whose suit he is arrested, well;

But he's in a suit of buff which 'rested him, that can I tell.

Will you send him, mistress, redemption, the money in his desk?

ADRIANA.

Go fetch it, sister. This I wonder at,

[Exit LUCIANA]

Thus he unknown to me should be in debt.—

Tell me, was he arrested on a band?

DROMIO OF SYRACUSE.

Not on a band, but on a stronger thing;

A chain, a chain: do you not hear it ring?

ADRIANA.

What, the chain?

DROMIO OF SYRACUSE.

No, no, the bell; 'tis time that I were gone.

It was two ere I left him, and now the clock strikes one.

ADRIANA.

The hours come back! that did I never hear.

DROMIO OF SYRACUSE.

O yes. If any hour meet a sergeant, 'a turns back for very fear.

ADRIANA.

As if time were in debt! how fondly dost thou reason!

DROMIO OF SYRACUSE.

Time is a very bankrupt, and owes more than he's worth to season.

Nay, he's a thief too: have you not heard men say

That Time comes stealing on by night and day?

If he be in debt and theft, and a sergeant in the way,

Hath he not reason to turn back an hour in a day?

[Enter LUCIANA.]

ADRIANA.

Go, Dromio, there's the money, bear it straight;

And bring thy master home immediately.—

Come, sister; I am press'd down with conceit-

Conceit my comfort and my injury.

[Exeunt.]

SCENE 3. The same.

[Enter ANTIPHOLUS OF SYRACUSE.]

ANTIPHOLUS OF SYRACUSE.

There's not a man I meet but doth salute me

As if I were their well-acquainted friend;

And every one doth call me by my name.

Some tender money to me, some invite me;

Some other give me thanks for kindnesses;

Some offer me commodities to buy;

Even now a tailor call'd me in his shop,

And show'd me silks that he had bought for me,

And therewithal took measure of my body.

Sure, these are but imaginary wiles,

And Lapland sorcerers inhabit here.

[Enter DROMIO OF SYRACUSE.]

DROMIO OF SYRACUSE.

Master, here's the gold you sent me for.

What, have you got the picture of old Adam new apparelled?

ANTIPHOLUS OF SYRACUSE.

What gold is this? What Adam dost thou mean?

DROMIO OF SYRACUSE. Not that Adam that kept the paradise, but that Adam that keeps the prison; he that goes in the calf's skin that was killed for the Prodigal; he that came behind you, sir, like an evil angel, and bid you forsake your liberty.

ANTIPHOLUS OF SYRACUSE.

I understand thee not.

DROMIO OF SYRACUSE. No? Why, 'tis a plain case: he that went like a bass-viol in a case of leather; the man, sir, that, when gentlemen are tired, gives them a sob, and 'rests them; he, sir, that takes pity on decayed men, and gives them suits of durance; he that sets up his rest to do more exploits with his mace than a morris-pike.

ANTIPHOLUS OF SYRACUSE.

What! thou mean'st an officer?

DROMIO OF SYRACUSE. Ay, sir,—the sergeant of the band: that brings any man to answer it that breaks his band; one that thinks a man always going to bed, and says 'God give you good rest!'

ANTIPHOLUS OF SYRACUSE. Well, sir, there rest in your foolery. Is there any ship puts forth to-night? may we be gone?

DROMIO OF SYRACUSE. Why, sir, I brought you word an hour since that the bark Expedition put forth to-night; and then were you hindered by the sergeant, to tarry for the hoy, Delay: here are the angels that you sent for to deliver you.

ANTIPHOLUS OF SYRACUSE.

The fellow is distract, and so am I;

And here we wander in illusions:

Some blessed power deliver us from hence!

[Enter a COURTEZAN.]

COURTEZAN.

Well met, well met, Master Antipholus.

I see, sir, you have found the goldsmith now:

Is that the chain you promis'd me to-day?

ANTIPHOLUS OF SYRACUSE.

Satan, avoid! I charge thee, tempt me not!

DROMIO OF SYRACUSE.

Master, is this Mistress Satan?

ANTIPHOLUS OF SYRACUSE.

It is the devil.

DROMIO OF SYRACUSE. Nay, she is worse,—she is the devil's dam; and here she comes in the habit of a light wench; and thereof comes that the wenches say 'God damn me!' That's as much to say 'God make me a light wench!' It is written they appear to men like angels of light: light is an effect of fire, and fire will burn; ergo, light wenches will burn: come not near her.

COURTEZAN.

Your man and you are marvellous merry, sir.

Will you go with me? We'll mend our dinner here.

DROMIO OF SYRACUSE.

Master, if you do; expect spoon-meat, or bespeak a long spoon.

ANTIPHOLUS OF SYRACUSE.

Why, Dromio?

DROMIO OF SYRACUSE.

Marry, he must have a long spoon that must eat with the devil.

ANTIPHOLUS OF SYRACUSE.

Avoid then, fiend! What tell'st thou me of supping?

Thou art, as you are all, a sorceress;

I conjure thee to leave me and be gone.

COURTEZAN.

Give me the ring of mine you had at dinner,

Or, for my diamond, the chain you promis'd,

And I'll be gone, sir, and not trouble you.

DROMIO OF SYRACUSE.

Some devils ask but the paring of one's nail,

A rush, a hair, a drop of blood, a pin,

A nut, a cherry-stone; but she, more covetous,

Would have a chain.

Master, be wise; an if you give it her,

The devil will shake her chain, and fright us with it.

COURTEZAN.

I pray you, sir, my ring, or else the chain;

I hope you do not mean to cheat me so.

ANTIPHOLUS OF SYRACUSE.

Avaunt, thou witch! Come, Dromio, let us go.

DROMIO OF SYRACUSE.

Fly pride, says the peacock: Mistress, that you know.

[Exeunt ANTIPHOLUS OF SYRACUSE and DROMIO OF
SYRACUSE.]

COURTEZAN.

Now, out of doubt, Antipholus is mad,

Else would he never so demean himself:

A ring he hath of mine worth forty ducats,

And for the same he promis'd me a chain;

Both one and other he denies me now:

The reason that I gather he is mad,—

Besides this present instance of his rage,—

Is a mad tale he told to-day at dinner,

Of his own doors being shut against his entrance.

Belike his wife, acquainted with his fits,

On purpose shut the doors against his way.

My way is now to hie home to his house,

And tell his wife that, being lunatic,

He rush'd into my house and took perforce

My ring away: this course I fittest choose,

For forty ducats is too much to lose.

[Exit.]

SCENE 4. The same.

[Enter ANTIPHOLUS OF EPHESUS and an OFFICER.]

ANTIPHOLUS OF EPHESUS.

Fear me not, man; I will not break away:

I'll give thee, ere I leave thee, so much money,

To warrant thee, as I am 'rested for.

My wife is in a wayward mood to-day;

And will not lightly trust the messenger

That I should be attach'd in Ephesus;

I tell you, 'twill sound harshly in her ears.

[Enter DROMIO OF EPHESUS, with a rope's end.]

Here comes my man: I think he brings the money.

How now, sir! have you that I sent you for?

DROMIO OF EPHESUS.

Here's that, I warrant you, will pay them all.

ANTIPHOLUS OF EPHESUS.

But where's the money?

DROMIO OF EPHESUS.

Why, sir, I gave the money for the rope.

ANTIPHOLUS OF EPHESUS.

Five hundred ducats, villain, for rope?

DROMIO OF EPHESUS.

I'll serve you, sir, five hundred at the rate.

ANTIPHOLUS OF EPHESUS.

To what end did I bid thee hie thee home?

DROMIO OF EPHESUS.

To a rope's end, sir; and to that end am I return'd.

ANTIPHOLUS OF EPHESUS.

And to that end, sir, I will welcome you.

[Beating him.]

OFFICER. Good sir, be patient.

DROMIO OF EPHESUS.

Nay, 'tis for me to be patient; I am in adversity.

OFFICER.

Good now, hold thy tongue.

DROMIO OF EPHESUS.

Nay, rather persuade him to hold his hands.

ANTIPHOLUS OF EPHESUS.

Thou whoreson senseless villain!

DROMIO OF EPHESUS.

I would I were senseless, sir, that I might not feel your blows.

ANTIPHOLUS OF EPHESUS.

Thou art sensible in nothing but blows, and so is an ass.

DROMIO OF EPHESUS. I am an ass indeed; you may prove it by my long 'ears. I have served him from the hour of my nativity to this instant, and have nothing at his hands for my service but blows: when I am cold he heats me with beating; when I am warm he cools me with beating. I am waked with it when I sleep; raised with it when I sit; driven out of doors with it when I go from home; welcomed home with it when I return: nay, I bear it on my shoulders as beggar wont her brat; and I think, when he hath lamed me, I shall beg with it from door to door.

ANTIPHOLUS OF EPHESUS.

Come, go along; my wife is coming yonder.

[Enter ADRIANA, LUCIANA, and the COURTEZAN, with PINCH and others.]

DROMIO OF EPHESUS. Mistress, 'respice finem,' respect your end; or rather, the prophesy, like the parrot, 'Beware the rope's-end.'

ANTIPHOLUS OF EPHESUS.

Wilt thou still talk?

[Beats him.]

COURTEZAN.

How say you now? is not your husband mad?

ADRIANA.

His incivility confirms no less.—

Good Doctor Pinch, you are a conjurer;

Establish him in his true sense again,

And I will please you what you will demand.

LUCIANA.

Alas, how fiery and how sharp he looks!

COURTEZAN.

Mark how he trembles in his ecstasy!

PINCH.

Give me your hand, and let me feel your pulse.

ANTIPHOLUS OF EPHESUS.

There is my hand, and let it feel your ear.

PINCH.

I charge thee, Satan, hous'd within this man,

To yield possession to my holy prayers,

And to thy state of darkness hie thee straight:

I conjure thee by all the saints in heaven.

ANTIPHOLUS OF EPHESUS.

Peace, doting wizard, peace; I am not mad.

ADRIANA.

O, that thou wert not, poor distressed soul!

ANTIPHOLUS OF EPHESUS.

You minion, you, are these your customers?

Did this companion with the saffron face

Revel and feast it at my house to-day,

Whilst upon me the guilty doors were shut,

And I denied to enter in my house?

ADRIANA.

O husband, God doth know you din'd at home,

Where would you had remain'd until this time,

Free from these slanders and this open shame!

ANTIPHOLUS OF EPHESUS.

I din'd at home! Thou villain, what sayest thou?

DROMIO OF EPHESUS.

Sir, sooth to say, you did not dine at home.

ANTIPHOLUS OF EPHESUS.

Were not my doors lock'd up and I shut out?

DROMIO OF EPHESUS.

Perdy, your doors were lock'd and you shut out.

ANTIPHOLUS OF EPHESUS.

And did not she herself revile me there?

DROMIO OF EPHESUS.

Sans fable, she herself revil'd you there.

ANTIPHOLUS OF EPHESUS.

Did not her kitchen-maid rail, taunt, and scorn me?

DROMIO OF EPHESUS.

Certes, she did: the kitchen-vestal scorn'd you.

ANTIPHOLUS OF EPHESUS.

And did not I in rage depart from thence?

DROMIO OF EPHESUS.

In verity, you did;—my bones bear witness,

That since have felt the vigour of his rage.

ADRIANA.

Is't good to soothe him in these contraries?

PINCH.

It is no shame; the fellow finds his vein,

And, yielding to him, humours well his frenzy.

ANTIPHOLUS OF EPHESUS.

Thou hast suborn'd the goldsmith to arrest me.

ADRIANA.

Alas! I sent you money to redeem you,

By Dromio here, who came in haste for it.

DROMIO OF EPHESUS.

Money by me! heart and goodwill you might,

But surely, master, not a rag of money.

ANTIPHOLUS OF EPHESUS.

Went'st not thou to her for purse of ducats?

ADRIANA.

He came to me, and I deliver'd it.

LUCIANA.

And I am witness with her that she did.

DROMIO OF EPHESUS.

God and the rope-maker, bear me witness

That I was sent for nothing but a rope!

PINCH.

Mistress, both man and master is possess'd;

I know it by their pale and deadly looks:

They must be bound, and laid in some dark room.

ANTIPHOLUS OF EPHESUS.

Say, wherefore didst thou lock me forth to-day?—

And why dost thou deny the bag of gold?

ADRIANA.

I did not, gentle husband, lock thee forth.

DROMIO OF EPHESUS.

And, gentle master, I receiv'd no gold;

But I confess, sir, that we were lock'd out.

ADRIANA.

Dissembling villain, thou speak'st false in both.

ANTIPHOLUS OF EPHESUS.

Dissembling harlot, thou art false in all;

And art confederate with a damned pack,

To make a loathsome abject scorn of me:

But with these nails I'll pluck out these false eyes

That would behold in me this shameful sport.

[PINCH and assistants bind ANTIPHOLUS OF EPHESUS and
DROMIO OF EPHESUS.]

ADRIANA.

O, bind him, bind him; let him not come near me.

PINCH.

More company;—the fiend is strong within him.

LUCIANA.

Ah me, poor man! how pale and wan he looks!

ANTIPHOLUS OF EPHESUS.

What, will you murder me? Thou gaoler, thou,

I am thy prisoner: wilt thou suffer them

To make a rescue?

OFFICER.

Masters, let him go:

He is my prisoner, and you shall not have him.

PINCH.

Go, bind this man, for he is frantic too.

ADRIANA.

What wilt thou do, thou peevish officer?

Hast thou delight to see a wretched man

Do outrage and displeasure to himself?

OFFICER.

He is my prisoner: if I let him go,

The debt he owes will be requir'd of me.

ADRIANA.

I will discharge thee ere I go from thee;

Bear me forthwith unto his creditor,

And, knowing how the debt grows, I will pay it.

Good master doctor, see him safe convey'd

Home to my house.—O most unhappy day!

ANTIPHOLUS OF EPHESUS.

O most unhappy strumpet!

DROMIO OF EPHESUS.

Master, I am here enter'd in bond for you.

ANTIPHOLUS OF EPHESUS.

Out on thee, villian! wherefore dost thou mad me?

DROMIO OF EPHESUS. Will you be bound for nothing? be mad, good master; cry, the devil.—

LUCIANA.

God help, poor souls, how idly do they talk!

ADRIANA.

Go bear him hence.—Sister, go you with me.—

> [Exeunt PINCH and Assistants, with ANTIPHOLUS OF EPHESUS and DROMIO OF EPHESUS.]

Say now, whose suit is he arrested at?

OFFICER.

One Angelo, a goldsmith; do you know him?

ADRIANA.

I know the man: what is the sum he owes?

OFFICER.

Two hundred ducats.

ADRIANA.

Say, how grows it due?

OFFICER.

Due for a chain your husband had of him.

ADRIANA.

He did bespeak a chain for me, but had it not.

COURTEZAN.

When as your husband, all in rage, to-day

Came to my house, and took away my ring,—

The ring I saw upon his finger now,—

Straight after did I meet him with a chain.

ADRIANA.

It may be so, but I did never see it:

Come, gaoler, bring me where the goldsmith is,

I long to know the truth hereof at large.

[Enter ANTIPHOLUS OF SYRACUSE, with his rapier drawn, and DROMIO OF SYRACUSE.]

LUCIANA.

God, for thy mercy! they are loose again.

ADRIANA.

And come with naked swords: let's call more help,

To have them bound again.

OFFICER.

Away, they'll kill us.

[Exeunt OFFICER, ADRIANA, and LUCIANA.]

ANTIPHOLUS OF SYRACUSE.

I see these witches are afraid of swords.

DROMIO OF SYRACUSE.

She that would be your wife now ran from you.

ANTIPHOLUS OF SYRACUSE.

Come to the Centaur; fetch our stuff from thence:

I long that we were safe and sound aboard.

DROMIO OF SYRACUSE. Faith, stay here this night; they will surely do us no harm; you saw they speak us fair, give us gold; methinks they are such a gentle nation that, but for the mountain of mad flesh that claims marriage of me, could find in my heart to stay here still and turn witch.

ANTIPHOLUS OF SYRACUSE.

I will not stay to-night for all the town;

Therefore away to get our stuff aboard.

[Exeunt.]

ACT V.

SCENE 1. The same.

[Enter MERCHANT and ANGELO.]

ANGELO.

I am sorry, sir, that I have hinder'd you;

But I protest he had the chain of me,

Though most dishonestly he doth deny it.

MERCHANT.

How is the man esteem'd here in the city?

ANGELO.

Of very reverend reputation, sir;

Of credit infinite, highly belov'd,

Second to none that lives here in the city:

His word might bear my wealth at any time.

MERCHANT.

Speak softly: yonder, as I think, he walks.

[Enter ANTIPHOLUS OF SYRACUSE and DROMIO OF SYRACUSE.]

ANGELO.

'Tis so; and that self chain about his neck

Which he forswore most monstrously to have.

Good sir, draw near to me, I'll speak to him.—

Signior Andpholus, I wonder much

That you would put me to this shame and trouble;

And, not without some scandal to yourself,

With circumstance and oaths so to deny

This chain, which now you wear so openly:

Beside the charge, the shame, imprisonment,

You have done wrong to this my honest friend;

Who, but for staying on our controversy,

Had hoisted sail and put to sea to-day;

This chain you had of me; can you deny it?

ANTIPHOLUS OF SYRACUSE.

I think I had: I never did deny it.

MERCHANT.

Yes, that you did, sir, and forswore it too.

ANTIPHOLUS OF SYRACUSE.

Who heard me to deny it or forswear it?

MERCHANT.

These ears of mine, thou know'st, did hear thee.

Fie on thee, wretch! 'tis pity that thou liv'st

To walk where any honest men resort.

ANTIPHOLUS OF SYRACUSE.

Thou art a villain to impeach me thus;

I'll prove mine honour and mine honesty

Against thee presently, if thou dar'st stand.

MERCHANT.

I dare, and do defy thee for a villain.

[They draw.]

[Enter ADRIANA, LUCIANA, COURTEZAN, and others.]

ADRIANA.

Hold, hurt him not, for God's sake; he is mad.

Some get within him, take his sword away:

Bind Dromio too, and bear them to my house.

DROMIO OF SYRACUSE.

Run, master, run; for God's sake, take a house.

This is some priory;—in, or we are spoil'd.

[Exeunt ANTIPHOLUS OF SYRACUSE and DROMIO OF
SYRACUSE to the priory.]

[Enter the ABBESS.]

ABBESS.

Be quiet, people. Wherefore throng you hither?

ADRIANA.

To fetch my poor distracted husband hence:

Let us come in, that we may bind him fast,

And bear him home for his recovery.

ANGELO.

I knew he was not in his perfect wits.

MERCHANT.

I am sorry now that I did draw on him.

ABBESS.

How long hath this possession held the man?

ADRIANA.

This week he hath been heavy, sour, sad,

And much different from the man he was:

But till this afternoon his passion

Ne'er brake into extremity of rage.

ABBESS.

Hath he not lost much wealth by wreck of sea?

Buried some dear friend? Hath not else his eye

Stray'd his affection in unlawful love?

A sin prevailing much in youthful men

Who give their eyes the liberty of gazing.

Which of these sorrows is he subject to?

ADRIANA.

To none of these, except it be the last;

Namely, some love that drew him oft from home.

ABBESS.

You should for that have reprehended him.

ADRIANA.

Why, so I did.

ABBESS.

Ay, but not rough enough.

ADRIANA.

As roughly as my modesty would let me.

ABBESS.

Haply in private.

ADRIANA.

And in assemblies too.

ABBESS.

Ay, but not enough.

ADRIANA.

It was the copy of our conference.

In bed, he slept not for my urging it;

At board, he fed not for my urging it;

Alone, it was the subject of my theme;

In company, I often glanced it;

Still did I tell him it was vile and bad.

ABBESS.

And thereof came it that the man was mad:

The venom clamours of a jealous woman

Poisons more deadly than a mad dog's tooth.

It seems his sleeps were hindered by thy railing:

And thereof comes it that his head is light.

Thou say'st his meat was sauc'd with thy upbraidings:

Unquiet meals make ill digestions;

Thereof the raging fire of fever bred;

And what's a fever but a fit of madness?

Thou say'st his sports were hinder'd by thy brawls:

Sweet recreation barr'd, what doth ensue

But moody and dull melancholy,—

Kinsman to grim and comfortless despair,—

And, at her heels, a huge infectious troop

Of pale distemperatures and foes to life?

In food, in sport, and life-preserving rest,

To be disturb'd would mad or man or beast:

The consequence is, then, thy jealous fits

Hath scar'd thy husband from the use of's wits.

LUCIANA.

She never reprehended him but mildly,

When he demean'd himself rough, rude, and wildly.—

Why bear you these rebukes, and answer not?

ADRIANA.

She did betray me to my own reproof.—

Good people, enter, and lay hold on him.

ABBESS.

No, not a creature enters in my house.

ADRIANA.

Then let your servants bring my husband forth.

ABBESS.

Neither: he took this place for sanctuary,

And it shall privilege him from your hands

Till I have brought him to his wits again,

Or lose my labour in assaying it.

ADRIANA.

I will attend my husband, be his nurse,

Diet his sickness, for it is my office,

And will have no attorney but myself;

And therefore let me have him home with me.

ABBESS.

Be patient; for I will not let him stir

Till I have used the approved means I have,

With wholesome syrups, drugs, and holy prayers,

To make of him a formal man again:

It is a branch and parcel of mine oath,

A charitable duty of my order;

Therefore depart, and leave him here with me.

ADRIANA.

I will not hence and leave my husband here;

And ill it doth beseem your holiness

To separate the husband and the wife.

ABBESS.

Be quiet, and depart: thou shalt not have him.

[Exit ABBESS.]

LUCIANA.

Complain unto the duke of this indignity.

ADRIANA.

Come, go; I will fall prostrate at his feet,

And never rise until my tears and prayers

Have won his grace to come in person hither

And take perforce my husband from the abbess.

MERCHANT.

By this, I think, the dial points at five:

Anon, I'm sure, the duke himself in person

Comes this way to the melancholy vale;

The place of death and sorry execution,

Behind the ditches of the abbey here.

ANGELO.

Upon what cause?

MERCHANT.

To see a reverend Syracusian merchant,

Who put unluckily into this bay

Against the laws and statutes of this town,

Beheaded publicly for his offence.

ANGELO.

See where they come: we will behold his death.

LUCIANA.

Kneel to the duke before he pass the abbey.

[Enter the DUKE, attended; AEGEON, bareheaded; with the HEADSMAN and other OFFICERS.]

DUKE.

Yet once again proclaim it publicly,

If any friend will pay the sum for him,

He shall not die; so much we tender him.

ADRIANA.

Justice, most sacred duke, against the abbess!

DUKE.

She is a virtuous and a reverend lady;

It cannot be that she hath done thee wrong.

ADRIANA.

May it please your grace, Antipholus, my husband,—

Who I made lord of me and all I had,

At your important letters,—this ill day

A most outrageous fit of madness took him;

That desp'rately he hurried through the street,—

With him his bondman all as mad as he,—

Doing displeasure to the citizens

By rushing in their houses, bearing thence

Rings, jewels, anything his rage did like.

Once did I get him bound and sent him home,

Whilst to take order for the wrongs I went,

That here and there his fury had committed.

Anon, I wot not by what strong escape,

He broke from those that had the guard of him;

And, with his mad attendant and himself,

Each one with ireful passion, with drawn swords,

Met us again, and, madly bent on us,

Chased us away; till, raising of more aid,

We came again to bind them: then they fled

Into this abbey, whither we pursued them:

And here the abbess shuts the gates on us,

And will not suffer us to fetch him out,

Nor send him forth that we may bear him hence.

Therefore, most gracious duke, with thy command

Let him be brought forth and borne hence for help.

DUKE.

Long since thy husband serv'd me in my wars;

And I to thee engag'd a prince's word,

When thou didst make him master of thy bed,

To do him all the grace and good I could.—

Go, some of you, knock at the abbey-gate,

And bid the lady abbess come to me:

I will determine this before I stir.

[Enter a SERVANT.]

SERVANT.

O mistress, mistress, shift and save yourself!

My master and his man are both broke loose,

Beaten the maids a-row, and bound the doctor;

Whose beard they have singed off with brands of fire;

And ever as it blazed they threw on him

Great pails of puddled mire to quench the hair:

My master preaches patience to him, while

His man with scissors nicks him like a fool:

And, sure, unless you send some present help,

Between them they will kill the conjurer.

ADRIANA.

Peace, fool, thy master and his man are here;

And that is false thou dost report to us.

SERVANT.

Mistress, upon my life, I tell you true:

I have not breath'd almost since I did see it.

He cries for you, and vows, if he can take you,

To scorch your face, and to disfigure you:

[Cry within.]

Hark, hark, I hear him, mistress; fly, be gone!

105

DUKE.

Come, stand by me; fear nothing. Guard with halberds.

ADRIANA.

Ah me, it is my husband! Witness you

That he is borne about invisible.

Even now we hous'd him in the abbey here,

And now he's there, past thought of human reason.

[Enter ANTIPHOLUS and DROMIO OF EPHESUS.]

ANTIPHOLUS OF EPHESUS.

Justice, most gracious duke; oh, grant me justice!

Even for the service that long since I did thee,

When I bestrid thee in the wars, and took

Deep scars to save thy life; even for the blood

That then I lost for thee, now grant me justice.

AEGEON.

Unless the fear of death doth make me dote,

I see my son Antipholus, and Dromio.

ANTIPHOLUS OF EPHESUS.

Justice, sweet prince, against that woman there.

She whom thou gav'st to me to be my wife;

That hath abused and dishonour'd me

Even in the strength and height of injury!

Beyond imagination is the wrong

That she this day hath shameless thrown on me.

DUKE.

Discover how, and thou shalt find me just.

ANTIPHOLUS OF EPHESUS.

This day, great duke, she shut the doors upon me,

While she with harlots feasted in my house.

DUKE.

A grievous fault. Say, woman, didst thou so?

ADRIANA.

No, my good lord;—myself, he, and my sister,

To-day did dine together. So befall my soul

As this is false he burdens me withal!

LUCIANA.

Ne'er may I look on day nor sleep on night

But she tells to your highness simple truth!

ANGELO.

O peflur'd woman! they are both forsworn.

In this the madman justly chargeth them.

ANTIPHOLUS OF EPHESUS.

My liege, I am advised what I say;

Neither disturb'd with the effect of wine,

Nor, heady-rash, provok'd with raging ire,

Albeit my wrongs might make one wiser mad.

This woman lock'd me out this day from dinner:

That goldsmith there, were he not pack'd with her,

Could witness it, for he was with me then;

Who parted with me to go fetch a chain.

Promising to bring it to the Porcupine,

Where Balthazar and I did dine together.

Our dinner done, and he not coming thither,

I went to seek him. In the street I met him,

And in his company that gentleman.

There did this perjur'd goldsmith swear me down,

That I this day of him receiv'd the chain,

Which, God he knows, I saw not: for the which

He did arrest me with an officer.

I did obey, and sent my peasant home

For certain ducats: he with none return'd.

Then fairly I bespoke the officer

To go in person with me to my house.

By the way we met

My wife, her sister, and a rabble more

Of vile confederates: along with them

They brought one Pinch; a hungry lean-faced villain,

A mere anatomy, a mountebank,

A threadbare juggler, and a fortune-teller;

A needy, hollow-ey'd, sharp-looking wretch;

A living dead man; this pernicious slave,

Forsooth, took on him as a conjurer;

And gazing in mine eyes, feeling my pulse,

And with no face, as 'twere, outfacing me,

Cries out, I was possess'd: then altogether

They fell upon me, bound me, bore me thence;

And in a dark and dankish vault at home

There left me and my man, both bound together;

Till, gnawing with my teeth my bonds in sunder,

I gain'd my freedom, and immediately

Ran hither to your grace; whom I beseech

To give me ample satisfaction

For these deep shames and great indignities.

ANGELO.

My lord, in truth, thus far I witness with him,

That he din'd not at home, but was lock'd out.

DUKE.

But had he such a chain of thee, or no?

ANGELO.

He had, my lord: and when he ran in here

These people saw the chain about his neck.

MERCHANT.

Besides, I will be sworn these ears of mine

Heard you confess you had the chain of him,

After you first forswore it on the mart,

And thereupon I drew my sword on you;

And then you fled into this abbey here,

From whence, I think, you are come by miracle.

ANTIPHOLUS OF EPHESUS.

I never came within these abbey walls,

Nor ever didst thou draw thy sword on me:

I never saw the chain, so help me heaven!

And this is false you burden me withal.

DUKE.

What an intricate impeach is this!

I think you all have drunk of Circe's cup.

If here you hous'd him, here he would have been:

If he were mad, he would not plead so coldly:—

You say he din'd at home: the goldsmith here

Denies that saying:—Sirrah, what say you?

DROMIO OF EPHESUS.

Sir, he dined with her there, at the Porcupine.

COURTEZAN.

He did; and from my finger snatch'd that ring.

ANTIPHOLUS OF EPHESUS.

'Tis true, my liege; this ring I had of her.

DUKE.

Saw'st thou him enter at the abbey here?

COURTEZAN.

As sure, my liege, as I do see your grace.

DUKE.

Why, this is strange:—Go call the abbess hither:

I think you are all mated, or stark mad.

[Exit an Attendant.]

AEGEON.

Most mighty Duke, vouchsafe me speak a word;

Haply, I see a friend will save my life

And pay the sum that may deliver me.

DUKE.

Speak freely, Syracusian, what thou wilt.

AEGEON.

Is not your name, sir, call'd Antipholus?

And is not that your bondman Dromio?

DROMIO OF EPHESUS.

Within this hour I was his bondman, sir,

But he, I thank him, gnaw'd in two my cords:

Now am I Dromio and his man unbound.

AEGEON.

I am sure you both of you remember me.

DROMIO OF EPHESUS.

Ourselves we do remember, sir, by you;

For lately we were bound as you are now.

You are not Pinch's patient, are you, sir?

AEGEON.

Why look you strange on me? you know me well.

ANTIPHOLUS OF EPHESUS.

I never saw you in my life, till now.

AEGEON.

Oh! grief hath chang'd me since you saw me last;

And careful hours with Time's deformed hand,

Have written strange defeatures in my face:

But tell me yet, dost thou not know my voice?

ANTIPHOLUS OF EPHESUS.

Neither.

AEGEON.

Dromio, nor thou?

DROMIO OF EPHESUS.

No, trust me, sir, nor I.

AEGEON.

I am sure thou dost.

DROMIO OF EPHESUS. Ay, sir, but I am sure I do not; and whatsoever a man denies, you are now bound to believe him.

AEGEON.

Not know my voice! O time's extremity!

Hast thou so crack'd and splitted my poor tongue,

In seven short years that here my only son

Knows not my feeble key of untun'd cares?

Though now this grained face of mine be hid

In sap-consuming winter's drizzled snow,

And all the conduits of my blood froze up,

Yet hath my night of life some memory,

My wasting lamps some fading glimmer left,

My dull deaf ears a little use to hear:

All these old witnesses,—I cannot err,—

Tell me thou art my son Antipholus.

ANTIPHOLUS OF EPHESUS.

I never saw my father in my life.

AEGEON.

But seven years since, in Syracusa, boy,

Thou know'st we parted; but perhaps, my son,

Thou sham'st to acknowledge me in misery.

ANTIPHOLUS OF EPHESUS.

The duke and all that know me in the city,

Can witness with me that it is not so:

I ne'er saw Syracusa in my life.

DUKE.

I tell thee, Syracusan, twenty years

Have I been patron to Antipholus,

During which time he ne'er saw Syracusa:

I see thy age and dangers make thee dote.

[Enter the ABBESS, with ANTIPHOLUS SYRACUSAN and DROMIO SYRACUSAN.]

ABBESS.

Most mighty duke, behold a man much wrong'd.

[All gather to see them.]

ADRIANA.

I see two husbands, or mine eyes deceive me.

DUKE.

One of these men is genius to the other;

And so of these. Which is the natural man,

And which the spirit? Who deciphers them?

DROMIO OF SYRACUSE.

I, sir, am Dromio; command him away.

DROMIO OF EPHESUS.

I, sir, am Dromio; pray let me stay.

ANTIPHOLUS OF SYRACUSE.

Aegeon, art thou not? or else his ghost?

DROMIO OF SYRACUSE.

O, my old master! who hath bound him here?

ABBESS.

Whoever bound him, I will loose his bonds,

And gain a husband by his liberty.—

Speak, old Aegeon, if thou be'st the man

That hadst a wife once called Aemilia,

That bore thee at a burden two fair sons:

O, if thou be'st the same Aegeon, speak,

And speak unto the same Aemilia!

AEGEON.

If I dream not, thou art Aemilia:

If thou art she, tell me where is that son

That floated with thee on the fatal raft?

ABBESS.

By men of Epidamnum, he and I,

And the twin Dromio, all were taken up:

But, by and by, rude fishermen of Corinth

By force took Dromio and my son from them,

And me they left with those of Epidamnum:

What then became of them I cannot tell;

I to this fortune that you see me in.

DUKE.

Why, here begins his morning story right:

These two Antipholus', these two so like,

And these two Dromios, one in semblance,—

Besides her urging of her wreck at sea,—

These are the parents to these children,

Which accidentally are met together.

Antipholus, thou cam'st from Corinth first?

ANTIPHOLUS OF SYRACUSE.

No, sir, not I; I came from Syracuse.

DUKE.

Stay, stand apart; I know not which is which.

ANTIPHOLUS OF EPHESUS.

I came from Corinth, my most gracious lord.

DROMIO OF EPHESUS.

And I with him.

ANTIPHOLUS OF EPHESUS.

Brought to this town by that most famous warrior,

Duke Menaphon, your most renowned uncle.

ADRIANA.

Which of you two did dine with me to-day?

ANTIPHOLUS OF SYRACUSE.

I, gentle mistress.

ADRIANA.

And are not you my husband?

ANTIPHOLUS OF EPHESUS.

No; I say nay to that.

ANTIPHOLUS OF SYRACUSE.

And so do I, yet did she call me so;

And this fair gentlewoman, her sister here,

Did call me brother.—What I told you then,

I hope I shall have leisure to make good;

If this be not a dream I see and hear.

ANGELO.

That is the chain, sir, which you had of me.

ANTIPHOLUS OF SYRACUSE.

I think it be, sir; I deny it not.

ANTIPHOLUS OF EPHESUS.

And you, sir, for this chain arrested me.

ANGELO.

I think I did, sir: I deny it not.

ADRIANA.

I sent you money, sir, to be your bail,

By Dromio; but I think he brought it not.

DROMIO OF EPHESUS.

No, none by me.

ANTIPHOLUS OF SYRACUSE.

This purse of ducats I receiv'd from you,

And Dromio my man did bring them me:

I see we still did meet each other's man,

And I was ta'en for him, and he for me,

And thereupon these errors are arose.

ANTIPHOLUS OF EPHESUS.

These ducats pawn I for my father here.

DUKE.

It shall not need; thy father hath his life.

COURTEZAN.

Sir, I must have that diamond from you.

ANTIPHOLUS OF EPHESUS.

There, take it; and much thanks for my good cheer.

ABBESS.

Renowned duke, vouchsafe to take the pains

To go with us into the abbey here,

And hear at large discoursed all our fortunes:—

And all that are assembled in this place,

That by this sympathized one day's error

Have suffer'd wrong, go, keep us company,

And we shall make full satisfaction—

Twenty-five years have I but gone in travail

Of you, my sons; nor till this present hour

My heavy burdens are delivered:—

The duke, my husband, and my children both,

And you the calendars of their nativity,

Go to a gossips' feast, and go with me;

After so long grief, such nativity!

DUKE.

With all my heart, I'll gossip at this feast.

> [Exeunt DUKE, ABBESS, AEGEON, Courtezan, Merchant,
> ANGELO, and Attendants.]

DROMIO OF SYRACUSE.

Master, shall I fetch your stuff from shipboard?

ANTIPHOLUS OF EPHESUS.

Dromio, what stuff of mine hast thou embark'd?

DROMIO OF SYRACUSE.

Your goods that lay at host, sir, in the Centaur.

ANTIPHOLUS OF SYRACUSE.

He speaks to me; I am your master, Dromio:

Come, go with us: we'll look to that anon:

Embrace thy brother there; rejoice with him.

> [Exeunt ANTIPHOLUS OF SYRACUSE and ANTIPHOLUS OF
> EPHESUS, ADRIANA, and LUCIANA.]

DROMIO OF SYRACUSE.

There is a fat friend at your master's house,

That kitchen'd me for you to-day at dinner:

She now shall be my sister, not my wife.

DROMIO OF EPHESUS.

Methinks you are my glass, and not my brother:

I see by you I am a sweet-faced youth.

Will you walk in to see their gossiping?

DROMIO OF SYRACUSE.

Not I, sir; you are my elder.

DROMIO OF EPHESUS.

That's a question; how shall we try it?

DROMIO OF SYRACUSE.

We'll draw cuts for the senior: till then, lead thou first.

DROMIO OF EPHESUS.

Nay, then, thus:

We came into the world like brother and brother:

And now let's go hand in hand, not one before another.

[Exeunt.]

MUCH ADO ABOUT NOTHING

Dramatis Personæ

DON PEDRO, Prince of Arragon.

DON JOHN, his bastard Brother.

CLAUDIO, a young Lord of Florence.

BENEDICK, a young Lord of Padua.

LEONATO, Governor of Messina.

ANTONIO, his Brother.

BALTHASAR, Servant to Don Pedro.

BORACHIO, follower of Don John.

CONRADE, follower of Don John.

DOGBERRY, a Constable.

VERGES, a Headborough.

FRIAR FRANCIS.

A Sexton.

A Boy.

HERO, Daughter to Leonato.

BEATRICE, Niece to Leonato.

MARGARET, Waiting gentlewoman attending on Hero.

URSULA, Waiting gentlewoman attending on Hero.

Messengers, Watch, Attendants, &c.

SCENE. Messina.

ACT I

SCENE I. Before Leonato's House.

Enter Leonato, Hero, Beatrice and others, with a Messenger.

LEONATO.

I learn in this letter that Don Pedro of Arragon comes this night to Messina.

MESSENGER.

He is very near by this: he was not three leagues off when I left him.

LEONATO.

How many gentlemen have you lost in this action?

MESSENGER.

But few of any sort, and none of name.

LEONATO.

A victory is twice itself when the achiever brings home full numbers. I find here that Don Pedro hath bestowed much honour on a young Florentine called Claudio.

MESSENGER.

Much deserved on his part, and equally remembered by Don Pedro. He hath borne himself beyond the promise of his age, doing in the figure of a lamb the feats of a lion: he hath indeed better bettered expectation than you must expect of me to tell you how.

LEONATO.

He hath an uncle here in Messina will be very much glad of it.

MESSENGER.

I have already delivered him letters, and there appears much joy in him; even so much that joy could not show itself modest enough without a badge of bitterness.

LEONATO.

Did he break out into tears?

MESSENGER.

In great measure.

LEONATO.

A kind overflow of kindness. There are no faces truer than those that are so washed; how much better is it to weep at joy than to joy at weeping!

BEATRICE.

I pray you, is Signior Mountanto returned from the wars or no?

MESSENGER.

I know none of that name, lady: there was none such in the army of any sort.

LEONATO.

What is he that you ask for, niece?

HERO.

My cousin means Signior Benedick of Padua.

MESSENGER.

O! he is returned, and as pleasant as ever he was.

BEATRICE.

He set up his bills here in Messina and challenged Cupid at the flight; and my uncle's fool, reading the challenge, subscribed for Cupid, and challenged him at the bird-bolt. I pray you, how many hath he killed and eaten in these wars? But how many hath he killed? for, indeed, I promised to eat all of his killing.

LEONATO.

Faith, niece, you tax Signior Benedick too much; but he'll be meet with you, I doubt it not.

MESSENGER.

He hath done good service, lady, in these wars.

BEATRICE.

You had musty victual, and he hath holp to eat it; he is a very valiant trencher-man; he hath an excellent stomach.

MESSENGER.

And a good soldier too, lady.

BEATRICE.

And a good soldier to a lady; but what is he to a lord?

MESSENGER.

A lord to a lord, a man to a man; stuffed with all honourable virtues.

BEATRICE.

It is so indeed; he is no less than a stuffed man; but for the stuffing,— well, we are all mortal.

LEONATO.

You must not, sir, mistake my niece. There is a kind of merry war betwixt Signior Benedick and her; they never meet but there's a skirmish of wit between them.

BEATRICE.

Alas! he gets nothing by that. In our last conflict four of his five wits went halting off, and now is the whole man governed with one! so that if he have wit enough to keep himself warm, let him bear it for a difference between himself and his horse; for it is all the wealth that he hath left to be known a reasonable creature. Who is his companion now? He hath every month a new sworn brother.

MESSENGER.

Is't possible?

BEATRICE.

Very easily possible: he wears his faith but as the fashion of his hat; it ever changes with the next block.

MESSENGER.

I see, lady, the gentleman is not in your books.

BEATRICE.

No; and he were, I would burn my study. But I pray you, who is his companion? Is there no young squarer now that will make a voyage with him to the devil?

MESSENGER.

He is most in the company of the right noble Claudio.

BEATRICE.

O Lord, he will hang upon him like a disease: he is sooner caught than the pestilence, and the taker runs presently mad. God help the noble Claudio! If he have caught the Benedick, it will cost him a thousand pound ere he be cured.

MESSENGER.

I will hold friends with you, lady.

BEATRICE.

Do, good friend.

LEONATO.

You will never run mad, niece.

BEATRICE.

No, not till a hot January.

MESSENGER.

Don Pedro is approached.

Enter Don Pedro, Don John, Claudio, Benedick, Balthasar and Others.

DON PEDRO.

Good Signior Leonato, you are come to meet your trouble: the fashion of the world is to avoid cost, and you encounter it.

LEONATO.

Never came trouble to my house in the likeness of your Grace, for trouble being gone, comfort should remain; but when you depart from me, sorrow abides and happiness takes his leave.

DON PEDRO.

You embrace your charge too willingly. I think this is your daughter.

LEONATO.

Her mother hath many times told me so.

BENEDICK.

Were you in doubt, sir, that you asked her?

LEONATO.

Signior Benedick, no; for then were you a child.

DON PEDRO.

You have it full, Benedick: we may guess by this what you are, being a man. Truly the lady fathers herself. Be happy, lady, for you are like an honourable father.

BENEDICK.

If Signior Leonato be her father, she would not have his head on her shoulders for all Messina, as like him as she is.

BEATRICE.

I wonder that you will still be talking, Signior Benedick: nobody marks you.

BENEDICK.

What! my dear Lady Disdain, are you yet living?

BEATRICE.

Is it possible Disdain should die while she hath such meet food to feed it as Signior Benedick? Courtesy itself must convert to disdain if you come in her presence.

BENEDICK.

Then is courtesy a turncoat. But it is certain I am loved of all ladies, only you excepted; and I would I could find in my heart that I had not a hard heart; for, truly, I love none.

BEATRICE.

A dear happiness to women: they would else have been troubled with a pernicious suitor. I thank God and my cold blood, I am of your humour for that. I had rather hear my dog bark at a crow than a man swear he loves me.

BENEDICK.

God keep your Ladyship still in that mind; so some gentleman or other shall scape a predestinate scratched face.

BEATRICE.

Scratching could not make it worse, and 'twere such a face as yours were.

BENEDICK.

Well, you are a rare parrot-teacher.

BEATRICE.

A bird of my tongue is better than a beast of yours.

BENEDICK.

I would my horse had the speed of your tongue, and so good a continuer. But keep your way, i' God's name; I have done.

BEATRICE.

You always end with a jade's trick: I know you of old.

DON PEDRO.

That is the sum of all, Leonato: Signior Claudio, and Signior Benedick, my dear friend Leonato hath invited you all. I tell him we shall stay here at the least a month, and he heartly prays some occasion may detain us longer: I dare swear he is no hypocrite, but prays from his heart.

LEONATO.

If you swear, my lord, you shall not be forsworn. [To Don John] Let me bid you welcome, my lord: being reconciled to the Prince your brother, I owe you all duty.

DON JOHN.

I thank you: I am not of many words, but I thank you.

LEONATO.

Please it your Grace lead on?

DON PEDRO.

Your hand, Leonato; we will go together.

[Exeunt all but Benedick and Claudio.]

CLAUDIO.

Benedick, didst thou note the daughter of Signior Leonato?

BENEDICK.

I noted her not; but I looked on her.

CLAUDIO.

Is she not a modest young lady?

BENEDICK.

Do you question me, as an honest man should do, for my simple true judgment; or would you have me speak after my custom, as being a professed tyrant to their sex?

CLAUDIO.

No; I pray thee speak in sober judgment.

BENEDICK.

Why, i' faith, methinks she's too low for a high praise, too brown for a fair praise, and too little for a great praise; only this commendation I can afford her, that were she other than she is, she were unhandsome, and being no other but as she is, I do not like her.

CLAUDIO.

Thou thinkest I am in sport: I pray thee tell me truly how thou likest her.

BENEDICK.

Would you buy her, that you enquire after her?

CLAUDIO.

Can the world buy such a jewel?

BENEDICK.

Yea, and a case to put it into. But speak you this with a sad brow, or do you play the flouting Jack, to tell us Cupid is a good hare-finder, and Vulcan a rare carpenter? Come, in what key shall a man take you, to go in the song?

CLAUDIO.

In mine eye she is the sweetest lady that ever I looked on.

BENEDICK.

I can see yet without spectacles and I see no such matter: there's her cousin and she were not possessed with a fury, exceeds her as much in beauty as the first of May doth the last of December. But I hope you have no intent to turn husband, have you?

CLAUDIO.

I would scarce trust myself, though I had sworn to the contrary, if Hero would be my wife.

BENEDICK.

Is't come to this, in faith? Hath not the world one man but he will wear his cap with suspicion? Shall I never see a bachelor of threescore again? Go to, i' faith; and thou wilt needs thrust thy neck into a yoke, wear the print of it and sigh away Sundays.

Re-enter Don Pedro.

Look! Don Pedro is returned to seek you.

DON PEDRO.

What secret hath held you here, that you followed not to Leonato's?

BENEDICK.

I would your Grace would constrain me to tell.

133

DON PEDRO.

I charge thee on thy allegiance.

BENEDICK.

You hear, Count Claudio: I can be secret as a dumb man; I would have you think so; but on my allegiance mark you this, on my allegiance: he is in love. With who? now that is your Grace's part. Mark how short his answer is: with Hero, Leonato's short daughter.

CLAUDIO.

If this were so, so were it uttered.

BENEDICK.

Like the old tale, my lord: 'it is not so, nor 'twas not so; but indeed, God forbid it should be so.'

CLAUDIO.

If my passion change not shortly, God forbid it should be otherwise.

DON PEDRO.

Amen, if you love her; for the lady is very well worthy.

CLAUDIO.

You speak this to fetch me in, my lord.

DON PEDRO.

By my troth, I speak my thought.

CLAUDIO.

And in faith, my lord, I spoke mine.

BENEDICK.

And by my two faiths and troths, my lord, I spoke mine.

CLAUDIO.

That I love her, I feel.

DON PEDRO.

That she is worthy, I know.

BENEDICK.

That I neither feel how she should be loved, nor know how she should be worthy, is the opinion that fire cannot melt out of me: I will die in it at the stake.

DON PEDRO.

Thou wast ever an obstinate heretic in the despite of beauty.

CLAUDIO.

And never could maintain his part but in the force of his will.

BENEDICK.

That a woman conceived me, I thank her; that she brought me up, I likewise give her most humble thanks; but that I will have a recheat winded in my forehead, or hang my bugle in an invisible baldrick, all women shall pardon me. Because I will not do them the wrong to mistrust any, I will do myself the right to trust none; and the fine is,—for the which I may go the finer,—I will live a bachelor.

DON PEDRO.

I shall see thee, ere I die, look pale with love.

BENEDICK.

With anger, with sickness, or with hunger, my lord; not with love: prove that ever I lose more blood with love than I will get again with drinking, pick out mine eyes with a ballad-maker's pen and hang me up at the door of a brothel-house for the sign of blind Cupid.

DON PEDRO.

Well, if ever thou dost fall from this faith, thou wilt prove a notable argument.

BENEDICK.

If I do, hang me in a bottle like a cat and shoot at me; and he that hits me, let him be clapped on the shoulder and called Adam.

DON PEDRO.

Well, as time shall try: 'In time the savage bull doth bear the yoke.'

BENEDICK.

The savage bull may; but if ever the sensible Benedick bear it, pluck off the bull's horns and set them in my forehead; and let me be vilely painted, and in such great letters as they write, 'Here is good horse to hire,' let them signify under my sign 'Here you may see Benedick the married man.'

CLAUDIO.

If this should ever happen, thou wouldst be horn-mad.

DON PEDRO.

Nay, if Cupid have not spent all his quiver in Venice, thou wilt quake for this shortly.

BENEDICK.

I look for an earthquake too then.

DON PEDRO.

Well, you will temporize with the hours. In the meantime, good Signior Benedick, repair to Leonato's: commend me to him and tell him I will not fail him at supper; for indeed he hath made great preparation.

BENEDICK.

I have almost matter enough in me for such an embassage; and so I commit you—

CLAUDIO.

To the tuition of God: from my house, if I had it,—

DON PEDRO.

The sixth of July: your loving friend, Benedick.

BENEDICK.

Nay, mock not, mock not. The body of your discourse is sometime guarded with fragments, and the guards are but slightly basted on neither: ere you flout old ends any further, examine your conscience: and so I leave you.

[Exit.]

CLAUDIO.

My liege, your Highness now may do me good.

DON PEDRO.

My love is thine to teach: teach it but how,

And thou shalt see how apt it is to learn

Any hard lesson that may do thee good.

CLAUDIO.

Hath Leonato any son, my lord?

DON PEDRO.

No child but Hero; she's his only heir.

Dost thou affect her, Claudio?

CLAUDIO.

O! my lord,

When you went onward on this ended action,

I looked upon her with a soldier's eye,

That lik'd, but had a rougher task in hand

Than to drive liking to the name of love;

But now I am return'd, and that war-thoughts

Have left their places vacant, in their rooms

Come thronging soft and delicate desires,

All prompting me how fair young Hero is,

Saying, I lik'd her ere I went to wars.

DON PEDRO.

Thou wilt be like a lover presently,

And tire the hearer with a book of words.

If thou dost love fair Hero, cherish it,

And I will break with her, and with her father,

And thou shalt have her. Was't not to this end

That thou began'st to twist so fine a story?

CLAUDIO.

How sweetly you do minister to love,

That know love's grief by his complexion!

But lest my liking might too sudden seem,

I would have salv'd it with a longer treatise.

DON PEDRO.

What need the bridge much broader than the flood?

The fairest grant is the necessity.

Look, what will serve is fit: 'tis once, thou lov'st,

And I will fit thee with the remedy.

I know we shall have revelling tonight:

I will assume thy part in some disguise,

And tell fair Hero I am Claudio;

And in her bosom I'll unclasp my heart,

And take her hearing prisoner with the force

And strong encounter of my amorous tale:

Then after to her father will I break;

And the conclusion is, she shall be thine.

In practice let us put it presently.

[Exeunt.]

SCENE II. A room in Leonato's house.

Enter Leonato and Antonio, meeting.

LEONATO.

How now, brother? Where is my cousin your son? Hath he provided this music?

ANTONIO.

He is very busy about it. But, brother, I can tell you strange news that you yet dreamt not of.

LEONATO.

Are they good?

ANTONIO.

As the event stamps them: but they have a good cover; they show well outward. The Prince and Count Claudio, walking in a thick-pleached alley in my orchard, were thus much overheard by a man of mine: the Prince discovered to Claudio that he loved my niece your daughter and meant to acknowledge it this night in a dance; and if he found her accordant, he meant to take the present time by the top and instantly break with you of it.

LEONATO.

Hath the fellow any wit that told you this?

ANTONIO.

A good sharp fellow: I will send for him; and question him yourself.

LEONATO.

No, no; we will hold it as a dream till it appear itself: but I will acquaint my daughter withal, that she may be the better prepared for an answer, if peradventure this be true. Go you and tell her of it.

[Several persons cross the stage.]

Cousins, you know what you have to do. O! I cry you mercy, friend; go you with me, and I will use your skill. Good cousin, have a care this busy time.

[Exeunt.]

SCENE III. Another room in Leonato's house.

Enter Don John and Conrade.

CONRADE.

What the good-year, my lord! why are you thus out of measure sad?

DON JOHN.

There is no measure in the occasion that breeds; therefore the sadness is without limit.

CONRADE.

You should hear reason.

DON JOHN.

And when I have heard it, what blessings brings it?

CONRADE.

If not a present remedy, at least a patient sufferance.

DON JOHN.

I wonder that thou (being as thou say'st thou art, born under Saturn) goest about to apply a moral medicine to a mortifying mischief. I cannot hide what I am: I must be sad when I have cause, and smile at no man's jests; eat when I have stomach, and wait for no man's leisure; sleep when I am drowsy, and tend on no man's business; laugh when I am merry, and claw no man in his humour.

CONRADE.

Yea; but you must not make the full show of this till you may do it without controlment. You have of late stood out against your brother, and he hath ta'en you newly into his grace; where it is impossible you should take true root but by the fair weather that you make yourself: it is needful that you frame the season for your own harvest.

DON JOHN.

I had rather be a canker in a hedge than a rose in his grace; and it better fits my blood to be disdained of all than to fashion a carriage to rob love from any: in this, though I cannot be said to be a flattering honest man, it must not be denied but I am a plain-dealing villain. I am trusted with a muzzle and enfranchised with a clog; therefore I have decreed not to sing in my cage. If I had my mouth, I would bite; if I had my liberty, I would do my liking: in the meantime, let me be that I am, and seek not to alter me.

CONRADE.

Can you make no use of your discontent?

DON JOHN.

I make all use of it, for I use it only. Who comes here?

Enter Borachio.

What news, Borachio?

BORACHIO.

I came yonder from a great supper: the Prince your brother is royally entertained by Leonato; and I can give you intelligence of an intended marriage.

DON JOHN.

Will it serve for any model to build mischief on? What is he for a fool that betroths himself to unquietness?

BORACHIO.

Marry, it is your brother's right hand.

DON JOHN.

Who? the most exquisite Claudio?

BORACHIO.

Even he.

DON JOHN.

A proper squire! And who, and who? which way looks he?

BORACHIO.

Marry, on Hero, the daughter and heir of Leonato.

DON JOHN.

A very forward March-chick! How came you to this?

BORACHIO.

Being entertained for a perfumer, as I was smoking a musty room, comes me the Prince and Claudio, hand in hand, in sad conference: I whipt me behind the arras, and there heard it agreed upon that the Prince should woo Hero for himself, and having obtained her, give her to Count Claudio.

DON JOHN.

Come, come; let us thither: this may prove food to my displeasure. That young start-up hath all the glory of my overthrow: if I can cross him any way, I bless myself every way. You are both sure, and will assist me?

CONRADE.

To the death, my lord.

DON JOHN.

Let us to the great supper: their cheer is the greater that I am subdued. Would the cook were of my mind! Shall we go to prove what's to be done?

BORACHIO.

We'll wait upon your Lordship.

[Exeunt.]

ACT II

SCENE I. A hall in Leonato's house.

Enter Leonato, Antonio, Hero, Beatrice and others.

LEONATO.

Was not Count John here at supper?

ANTONIO.

I saw him not.

BEATRICE.

How tartly that gentleman looks! I never can see him but I am heart-burned an hour after.

HERO.

He is of a very melancholy disposition.

BEATRICE.

He were an excellent man that were made just in the mid-way between him and Benedick: the one is too like an image, and says nothing; and the other too like my lady's eldest son, evermore tattling.

LEONATO.

Then half Signior Benedick's tongue in Count John's mouth, and half Count John's melancholy in Signior Benedick's face—

BEATRICE.

With a good leg and a good foot, uncle, and money enough in his purse, such a man would win any woman in the world if a' could get her good will.

LEONATO.

By my troth, niece, thou wilt never get thee a husband, if thou be so shrewd of thy tongue.

ANTONIO.

In faith, she's too curst.

BEATRICE.

Too curst is more than curst: I shall lessen God's sending that way; for it is said, 'God sends a curst cow short horns;' but to a cow too curst he sends none.

LEONATO.

So, by being too curst, God will send you no horns?

BEATRICE.

Just, if he send me no husband; for the which blessing I am at him upon my knees every morning and evening. Lord! I could not endure a husband with a beard on his face: I had rather lie in the woollen.

LEONATO.

You may light on a husband that hath no beard.

BEATRICE.

What should I do with him? dress him in my apparel and make him my waiting gentlewoman? He that hath a beard is more than a youth, and he that hath no beard is less than a man; and he that is more than a youth is not for me; and he that is less than a man, I am not for him: therefore I will even take sixpence in earnest of the bear-ward, and lead his apes into hell.

LEONATO.

Well then, go you into hell?

BEATRICE.

No; but to the gate; and there will the Devil meet me, like an old cuckold, with horns on his head, and say, 'Get you to heaven, Beatrice, get you to heaven; here's no place for you maids.' So deliver I up my apes, and away to Saint Peter for the heavens: he shows me where the bachelors sit, and there live we as merry as the day is long.

ANTONIO.

[To Hero.] Well, niece, I trust you will be ruled by your father.

BEATRICE.

Yes, faith; it is my cousin's duty to make curtsy, and say, 'Father, as it please you:'— but yet for all that, cousin, let him be a handsome fellow, or else make another curtsy, and say, 'Father, as it please me.'

LEONATO.

Well, niece, I hope to see you one day fitted with a husband.

BEATRICE.

Not till God make men of some other metal than earth. Would it not grieve a woman to be over-mastered with a piece of valiant dust? to make an account of her life to a clod of wayward marl? No, uncle, I'll none: Adam's sons are my brethren; and truly, I hold it a sin to match in my kindred.

LEONATO.

Daughter, remember what I told you: if the Prince do solicit you in that kind, you know your answer.

BEATRICE.

The fault will be in the music, cousin, if you be not wooed in good time: if the Prince be too important, tell him there is measure in everything, and so dance out the answer. For, hear me, Hero: wooing, wedding, and repenting is as a Scotch jig, a measure, and a cinquepace: the first suit is hot and hasty, like a Scotch jig, and full as fantastical; the wedding, mannerly modest, as a measure, full of state and ancientry; and then comes Repentance, and with his bad legs, falls into the cinquepace faster and faster, till he sink into his grave.

LEONATO.

Cousin, you apprehend passing shrewdly.

BEATRICE.

I have a good eye, uncle: I can see a church by daylight.

LEONATO.

The revellers are entering, brother: make good room.

Enter Don Pedro, Claudio, Benedick, Balthasar, Don John, Borachio, Margaret, Ursula and Others, masked.

DON PEDRO.

Lady, will you walk about with your friend?

HERO.

So you walk softly and look sweetly and say nothing, I am yours for the walk; and especially when I walk away.

DON PEDRO.

With me in your company?

HERO.

I may say so, when I please.

DON PEDRO.

And when please you to say so?

HERO.

When I like your favour; for God defend the lute should be like the case!

DON PEDRO.

My visor is Philemon's roof; within the house is Jove.

HERO.

Why, then, your visor should be thatch'd.

DON PEDRO.

Speak low, if you speak love.

[Takes her aside.]

BALTHASAR.

Well, I would you did like me.

MARGARET.

So would not I, for your own sake; for I have many ill qualities.

BALTHASAR.

Which is one?

MARGARET.

I say my prayers aloud.

BALTHASAR.

I love you the better; the hearers may cry Amen.

MARGARET.

God match me with a good dancer!

BALTHASAR.

Amen.

MARGARET.

And God keep him out of my sight when the dance is done! Answer, clerk.

BALTHASAR.

No more words: the clerk is answered.

URSULA.

I know you well enough: you are Signior Antonio.

ANTONIO.

At a word, I am not.

URSULA.

I know you by the waggling of your head.

ANTONIO.

To tell you true, I counterfeit him.

URSULA.

You could never do him so ill-well, unless you were the very man. Here's his dry hand up and down: you are he, you are he.

ANTONIO.

At a word, I am not.

URSULA.

Come, come; do you think I do not know you by your excellent wit? Can virtue hide itself? Go to, mum, you are he: graces will appear, and there's an end.

BEATRICE.

Will you not tell me who told you so?

BENEDICK.

No, you shall pardon me.

BEATRICE.

Nor will you not tell me who you are?

BENEDICK.

Not now.

BEATRICE.

That I was disdainful, and that I had my good wit out of the 'Hundred Merry Tales.' Well, this was Signior Benedick that said so.

BENEDICK.

What's he?

BEATRICE.

I am sure you know him well enough.

BENEDICK.

Not I, believe me.

BEATRICE.

Did he never make you laugh?

BENEDICK.

I pray you, what is he?

BEATRICE.

Why, he is the Prince's jester: a very dull fool; only his gift is in devising impossible slanders: none but libertines delight in him; and the commendation is not in his wit, but in his villainy; for he both pleases men and angers them, and then they laugh at him and beat him. I am sure he is in the fleet: I would he had boarded me!

BENEDICK.

When I know the gentleman, I'll tell him what you say.

BEATRICE.

Do, do: he'll but break a comparison or two on me; which, peradventure not marked or not laughed at, strikes him into melancholy; and then there's a partridge wing saved, for the fool will eat no supper that night. [Music within.] We must follow the leaders.

BENEDICK.

In every good thing.

BEATRICE.

Nay, if they lead to any ill, I will leave them at the next turning.

[Dance. Then exeunt all but Don John, Borachio and Claudio.]

DON JOHN.

Sure my brother is amorous on Hero, and hath withdrawn her father to break with him about it. The ladies follow her and but one visor remains.

BORACHIO.

And that is Claudio: I know him by his bearing.

DON JOHN.

Are you not Signior Benedick?

CLAUDIO.

You know me well; I am he.

DON JOHN.

Signior, you are very near my brother in his love: he is enamoured on Hero; I pray you, dissuade him from her; she is no equal for his birth: you may do the part of an honest man in it.

CLAUDIO.

How know you he loves her?

DON JOHN.

I heard him swear his affection.

BORACHIO.

So did I too; and he swore he would marry her tonight.

DON JOHN.

Come, let us to the banquet.

[Exeunt Don John and Borachio.]

CLAUDIO.

Thus answer I in name of Benedick,

But hear these ill news with the ears of Claudio.

'Tis certain so; the Prince wooes for himself.

Friendship is constant in all other things

Save in the office and affairs of love:

Therefore all hearts in love use their own tongues;

Let every eye negotiate for itself

And trust no agent; for beauty is a witch

Against whose charms faith melteth into blood.

This is an accident of hourly proof,

Which I mistrusted not. Farewell, therefore, Hero!

Re-enter Benedick.

BENEDICK.

Count Claudio?

CLAUDIO.

Yea, the same.

BENEDICK.

Come, will you go with me?

CLAUDIO.

Whither?

BENEDICK.

Even to the next willow, about your own business, Count. What fashion will you wear the garland of? About your neck, like a usurer's chain? or under your arm, like a lieutenant's scarf? You must wear it one way, for the Prince hath got your Hero.

CLAUDIO.

I wish him joy of her.

BENEDICK.

Why, that's spoken like an honest drovier: so they sell bullocks. But did you think the Prince would have served you thus?

CLAUDIO.

I pray you, leave me.

BENEDICK.

Ho! now you strike like the blind man: 'twas the boy that stole your meat, and you'll beat the post.

CLAUDIO.

If it will not be, I'll leave you.

[Exit.]

BENEDICK.

Alas! poor hurt fowl. Now will he creep into sedges. But, that my Lady Beatrice should know me, and not know me! The Prince's fool! Ha! it may be I go under that title because I am merry. Yea, but so I am apt to do myself wrong; I am not so reputed: it is the base though bitter disposition of Beatrice that puts the world into her person, and so gives me out. Well, I'll be revenged as I may.

Re-enter Don Pedro.

DON PEDRO.

Now, signior, where's the Count? Did you see him?

BENEDICK.

Troth, my lord, I have played the part of Lady Fame. I found him here as melancholy as a lodge in a warren. I told him, and I think I told him true, that your Grace had got the good will of this young lady; and I offered him my company to a willow tree, either to make him a garland, as being forsaken, or to bind him up a rod, as being worthy to be whipped.

DON PEDRO.

To be whipped! What's his fault?

BENEDICK.

The flat transgression of a school-boy, who, being overjoy'd with finding a bird's nest, shows it his companion, and he steals it.

DON PEDRO.

Wilt thou make a trust a transgression? The transgression is in the stealer.

BENEDICK.

Yet it had not been amiss the rod had been made, and the garland too; for the garland he might have worn himself, and the rod he might have bestowed on you, who, as I take it, have stolen his bird's nest.

DON PEDRO.

I will but teach them to sing, and restore them to the owner.

BENEDICK.

If their singing answer your saying, by my faith, you say honestly.

DON PEDRO.

The Lady Beatrice hath a quarrel to you: the gentleman that danced with her told her she is much wronged by you.

BENEDICK.

O! she misused me past the endurance of a block: an oak but with one green leaf on it would have answered her: my very visor began to assume life and scold with her. She told me, not thinking I had been myself, that I was the Prince's jester, that I was duller than a great thaw; huddling jest upon jest with such impossible conveyance upon me, that I stood like a man at a mark, with a whole army shooting at me. She speaks poniards, and every word stabs: if her breath were as terrible as her terminations, there were no living near her; she would infect to the north star. I would not marry her, though she were endowed with all that Adam had left him before he transgressed: she would have made Hercules have turned spit, yea, and have cleft his club to make the fire too. Come, talk not of her; you shall find her the infernal Ate in good apparel. I would to God some scholar would conjure her, for certainly, while she is here, a man may live as quiet in hell as in a sanctuary; and people sin upon purpose because they would go thither; so indeed, all disquiet, horror and perturbation follow her.

Re-enter Claudio, Beatrice, Hero and Leonato.

DON PEDRO.

Look! here she comes.

BENEDICK.

Will your Grace command me any service to the world's end? I will go on the slightest errand now to the Antipodes that you can devise to send me on; I will fetch you a toothpicker now from the furthest inch of Asia; bring you the length of Prester John's foot; fetch you a hair off the Great Cham's beard; do you any embassage to the Pygmies, rather than hold three words' conference with this harpy. You have no employment for me?

DON PEDRO.

None, but to desire your good company.

BENEDICK.

O God, sir, here's a dish I love not: I cannot endure my Lady Tongue.

[Exit.]

DON PEDRO.

Come, lady, come; you have lost the heart of Signior Benedick.

BEATRICE.

Indeed, my lord, he lent it me awhile; and I gave him use for it, a double heart for a single one: marry, once before he won it of me with false dice, therefore your Grace may well say I have lost it.

DON PEDRO.

You have put him down, lady, you have put him down.

BEATRICE.

So I would not he should do me, my lord, lest I should prove the mother of fools. I have brought Count Claudio, whom you sent me to seek.

DON PEDRO.

Why, how now, Count! wherefore are you sad?

CLAUDIO.

Not sad, my lord.

DON PEDRO.

How then? Sick?

CLAUDIO.

Neither, my lord.

BEATRICE.

The Count is neither sad, nor sick, nor merry, nor well; but civil Count, civil as an orange, and something of that jealous complexion.

157

DON PEDRO.

I' faith, lady, I think your blazon to be true; though, I'll be sworn, if he be so, his conceit is false. Here, Claudio, I have wooed in thy name, and fair Hero is won; I have broke with her father, and, his good will obtained; name the day of marriage, and God give thee joy!

LEONATO.

Count, take of me my daughter, and with her my fortunes: his Grace hath made the match, and all grace say Amen to it!

BEATRICE.

Speak, Count, 'tis your cue.

CLAUDIO.

Silence is the perfectest herald of joy: I were but little happy, if I could say how much. Lady, as you are mine, I am yours: I give away myself for you and dote upon the exchange.

BEATRICE.

Speak, cousin; or, if you cannot, stop his mouth with a kiss, and let not him speak neither.

DON PEDRO.

In faith, lady, you have a merry heart.

BEATRICE.

Yea, my lord; I thank it, poor fool, it keeps on the windy side of care. My cousin tells him in his ear that he is in her heart.

CLAUDIO.

And so she doth, cousin.

BEATRICE.

Good Lord, for alliance! Thus goes everyone to the world but I, and I am sunburnt. I may sit in a corner and cry heigh-ho for a husband!

DON PEDRO.

Lady Beatrice, I will get you one.

BEATRICE.

I would rather have one of your father's getting. Hath your Grace ne'er a brother like you? Your father got excellent husbands, if a maid could come by them.

DON PEDRO.

Will you have me, lady?

BEATRICE.

No, my lord, unless I might have another for working days: your Grace is too costly to wear every day. But, I beseech your Grace, pardon me; I was born to speak all mirth and no matter.

DON PEDRO.

Your silence most offends me, and to be merry best becomes you; for out of question, you were born in a merry hour.

BEATRICE.

No, sure, my lord, my mother cried; but then there was a star danced, and under that was I born. Cousins, God give you joy!

LEONATO.

Niece, will you look to those things I told you of?

BEATRICE.

I cry you mercy, uncle. By your Grace's pardon.

[Exit.]

DON PEDRO.

By my troth, a pleasant spirited lady.

LEONATO.

There's little of the melancholy element in her, my lord: she is never sad but when she sleeps; and not ever sad then, for I have heard my daughter say, she hath often dreamed of unhappiness and waked herself with laughing.

DON PEDRO.

She cannot endure to hear tell of a husband.

LEONATO.

O! by no means: she mocks all her wooers out of suit.

DON PEDRO.

She were an excellent wife for Benedick.

LEONATO.

O Lord! my lord, if they were but a week married, they would talk themselves mad.

DON PEDRO.

Count Claudio, when mean you to go to church?

CLAUDIO.

Tomorrow, my lord. Time goes on crutches till love have all his rites.

LEONATO.

Not till Monday, my dear son, which is hence a just seven-night; and a time too brief too, to have all things answer my mind.

DON PEDRO.

Come, you shake the head at so long a breathing; but, I warrant thee, Claudio, the time shall not go dully by us. I will in the interim undertake one of Hercules' labours, which is, to bring Signior Benedick and the Lady

Beatrice into a mountain of affection the one with the other. I would fain have it a match; and I doubt not but to fashion it, if you three will but minister such assistance as I shall give you direction.

LEONATO.

My lord, I am for you, though it cost me ten nights' watchings.

CLAUDIO.

And I, my lord.

DON PEDRO.

And you too, gentle Hero?

HERO.

I will do any modest office, my lord, to help my cousin to a good husband.

DON PEDRO.

And Benedick is not the unhopefullest husband that I know. Thus far can I praise him; he is of a noble strain, of approved valour, and confirmed honesty. I will teach you how to humour your cousin, that she shall fall in love with Benedick; and I, with your two helps, will so practise on Benedick that, in despite of his quick wit and his queasy stomach, he shall fall in love with Beatrice. If we can do this, Cupid is no longer an archer: his glory shall be ours, for we are the only love-gods. Go in with me, and I will tell you my drift.

[Exeunt.]

SCENE II. Another room in Leonato's house.

Enter Don John and Borachio.

DON JOHN.

It is so; the Count Claudio shall marry the daughter of Leonato.

BORACHIO.

Yea, my lord; but I can cross it.

DON JOHN.

Any bar, any cross, any impediment will be medicinable to me: I am sick in displeasure to him, and whatsoever comes athwart his affection ranges evenly with mine. How canst thou cross this marriage?

BORACHIO.

Not honestly, my lord; but so covertly that no dishonesty shall appear in me.

DON JOHN.

Show me briefly how.

BORACHIO.

I think I told your lordship, a year since, how much I am in the favour of Margaret, the waiting gentlewoman to Hero.

DON JOHN.

I remember.

BORACHIO.

I can, at any unseasonable instant of the night, appoint her to look out at her lady's chamber window.

DON JOHN.

What life is in that, to be the death of this marriage?

BORACHIO.

The poison of that lies in you to temper. Go you to the Prince your brother; spare not to tell him, that he hath wronged his honour in marrying the renowned Claudio,—whose estimation do you mightily hold up,—to a contaminated stale, such a one as Hero.

DON JOHN.

What proof shall I make of that?

BORACHIO.

Proof enough to misuse the Prince, to vex Claudio, to undo Hero, and kill Leonato. Look you for any other issue?

DON JOHN.

Only to despite them, I will endeavour anything.

BORACHIO.

Go then; find me a meet hour to draw Don Pedro and the Count Claudio alone: tell them that you know that Hero loves me; intend a kind of zeal both to the Prince and Claudio, as—in love of your brother's honour, who hath made this match, and his friend's reputation, who is thus like to be cozened with the semblance of a maid,—that you have discovered thus. They will scarcely believe this without trial: offer them instances, which shall bear no less likelihood than to see me at her chamber window, hear me call Margaret Hero, hear Margaret term me Claudio; and bring them to see this the very night before the intended wedding: for in the meantime I will so fashion the matter that Hero shall be absent; and there shall appear such seeming truth of Hero's disloyalty, that jealousy shall be called assurance, and all the preparation overthrown.

DON JOHN.

Grow this to what adverse issue it can, I will put it in practice. Be cunning in the working this, and thy fee is a thousand ducats.

BORACHIO.

Be you constant in the accusation, and my cunning shall not shame me.

DON JOHN.

I will presently go learn their day of marriage.

[Exeunt.]

SCENE III. Leonato's Garden.

Enter Benedick.

BENEDICK.

Boy!

Enter a Boy.

BOY.

Signior?

BENEDICK.

In my chamber window lies a book; bring it hither to me in the orchard.

BOY.

I am here already, sir.

BENEDICK.

I know that; but I would have thee hence, and here again.

[Exit Boy.]

I do much wonder that one man, seeing how much another man is a fool when he dedicates his behaviours to love, will, after he hath laughed at such shallow follies in others, become the argument of his own scorn by falling in love: and such a man is Claudio. I have known, when there was no music with him but the drum and the fife; and now had he rather hear the tabor and the pipe: I have known when he would have walked ten mile afoot to see a good armour; and now will he lie ten nights awake, carving the fashion of a new doublet. He was wont to speak plain and to the purpose, like an honest man and a soldier; and now is he turned orthography; his words are a very fantastical banquet, just so many strange dishes. May I be so converted, and see with these eyes? I cannot tell; I think not: I will not be sworn but love may transform me to an oyster; but I'll take my oath on it, till he have made an oyster of me, he shall never make me such a fool. One woman is fair, yet I am well; another is wise, yet I am well; another virtuous, yet I am well; but till all graces be in one woman, one woman shall not come in my grace. Rich she shall be, that's certain; wise, or I'll none; virtuous, or I'll never cheapen her; fair, or I'll never look on her; mild, or come not near me; noble, or not I for an angel; of good discourse, an excellent musician, and her hair shall be of what colour it please God. Ha! the Prince and Monsieur Love! I will hide me in the arbour.

[Withdraws.]

Enter Don Pedro, Leonato and Claudio, followed by Balthasar and Musicians.

DON PEDRO.

Come, shall we hear this music?

CLAUDIO.

Yea, my good lord. How still the evening is,

As hush'd on purpose to grace harmony!

DON PEDRO.

See you where Benedick hath hid himself?

CLAUDIO.

O! very well, my lord: the music ended,

We'll fit the kid-fox with a penny-worth.

DON PEDRO.

Come, Balthasar, we'll hear that song again.

BALTHASAR.

O! good my lord, tax not so bad a voice

To slander music any more than once.

DON PEDRO.

It is the witness still of excellency,

To put a strange face on his own perfection.

I pray thee, sing, and let me woo no more.

BALTHASAR.

Because you talk of wooing, I will sing;

Since many a wooer doth commence his suit

To her he thinks not worthy; yet he wooes;

Yet will he swear he loves.

DON PEDRO.

Nay, pray thee come;

Or if thou wilt hold longer argument,

Do it in notes.

BALTHASAR.

Note this before my notes;

There's not a note of mine that's worth the noting.

DON PEDRO.

Why these are very crotchets that he speaks;

Notes, notes, forsooth, and nothing!

[Music.]

BENEDICK.

Now, divine air! now is his soul ravished! Is it not strange that sheep's guts should hale souls out of men's bodies? Well, a horn for my money, when all's done.

167

BALTHASAR [sings.]

Sigh no more, ladies, sigh no more,

  Men were deceivers ever;

One foot in sea, and one on shore,

  To one thing constant never.

    Then sigh not so, but let them go,

  And be you blithe and bonny,

Converting all your sounds of woe

  Into Hey nonny, nonny.

Sing no more ditties, sing no mo

  Of dumps so dull and heavy;

The fraud of men was ever so,

  Since summer first was leavy.

    Then sigh not so, but let them go,

  And be you blithe and bonny,

Converting all your sounds of woe

  Into Hey nonny, nonny.

DON PEDRO.

By my troth, a good song.

BALTHASAR.

And an ill singer, my lord.

DON PEDRO.

Ha, no, no, faith; thou singest well enough for a shift.

BENEDICK.

[Aside] And he had been a dog that should have howled thus, they would have hanged him; and I pray God his bad voice bode no mischief. I had as lief have heard the night-raven, come what plague could have come after it.

DON PEDRO. Yea, marry; dost thou hear, Balthasar? I pray thee, get us some excellent music, for tomorrow night we would have it at the Lady Hero's chamber window.

BALTHASAR.

The best I can, my lord.

DON PEDRO.

Do so: farewell.

[Exeunt Balthasar and Musicians.]

Come hither, Leonato: what was it you told me of today, that your niece Beatrice was in love with Signior Benedick?

CLAUDIO.

O! ay:—[Aside to Don Pedro] Stalk on, stalk on; the fowl sits. I did never think that lady would have loved any man.

LEONATO.

No, nor I neither; but most wonderful that she should so dote on Signior Benedick, whom she hath in all outward behaviours seemed ever to abhor.

BENEDICK.

[Aside] Is't possible? Sits the wind in that corner?

LEONATO.

By my troth, my lord, I cannot tell what to think of it but that she loves him with an enraged affection: it is past the infinite of thought.

DON PEDRO.

Maybe she doth but counterfeit.

CLAUDIO.

Faith, like enough.

LEONATO.

O God! counterfeit! There was never counterfeit of passion came so near the life of passion as she discovers it.

DON PEDRO.

Why, what effects of passion shows she?

CLAUDIO.

[Aside] Bait the hook well: this fish will bite.

LEONATO.

What effects, my lord? She will sit you; [To Claudio] You heard my daughter tell you how.

CLAUDIO.

She did, indeed.

DON PEDRO.

How, how, I pray you? You amaze me: I would have thought her spirit had been invincible against all assaults of affection.

LEONATO.

I would have sworn it had, my lord; especially against Benedick.

BENEDICK.

[Aside] I should think this a gull, but that the white-bearded fellow speaks it: knavery cannot, sure, hide itself in such reverence.

170

CLAUDIO.

[Aside] He hath ta'en the infection: hold it up.

DON PEDRO.

Hath she made her affection known to Benedick?

LEONATO.

No; and swears she never will: that's her torment.

CLAUDIO.

'Tis true, indeed; so your daughter says: 'Shall I,' says she, 'that have so oft encountered him with scorn, write to him that I love him?'

LEONATO.

This says she now when she is beginning to write to him; for she'll be up twenty times a night, and there will she sit in her smock till she have writ a sheet of paper: my daughter tells us all.

CLAUDIO.

Now you talk of a sheet of paper, I remember a pretty jest your daughter told us of.

LEONATO.

O! when she had writ it, and was reading it over, she found Benedick and Beatrice between the sheet?

CLAUDIO.

That.

LEONATO.

O! she tore the letter into a thousand halfpence; railed at herself, that she should be so immodest to write to one that she knew would flout her: 'I measure him,' says she, 'by my own spirit; for I should flout him, if he writ to me; yea, though I love him, I should.'

CLAUDIO.

Then down upon her knees she falls, weeps, sobs, beats her heart, tears her hair, prays, curses; 'O sweet Benedick! God give me patience!'

LEONATO.

She doth indeed; my daughter says so; and the ecstasy hath so much overborne her, that my daughter is sometimes afeard she will do a desperate outrage to herself. It is very true.

DON PEDRO.

It were good that Benedick knew of it by some other, if she will not discover it.

CLAUDIO.

To what end? he would make but a sport of it and torment the poor lady worse.

DON PEDRO.

And he should, it were an alms to hang him. She's an excellent sweet lady, and, out of all suspicion, she is virtuous.

CLAUDIO.

And she is exceeding wise.

DON PEDRO.

In everything but in loving Benedick.

LEONATO.

O! my lord, wisdom and blood combating in so tender a body, we have ten proofs to one that blood hath the victory. I am sorry for her, as I have just cause, being her uncle and her guardian.

DON PEDRO.

I would she had bestowed this dotage on me; I would have daffed all other respects and made her half myself. I pray you, tell Benedick of it, and hear what he will say.

LEONATO.

Were it good, think you?

CLAUDIO.

Hero thinks surely she will die; for she says she will die if he love her not, and she will die ere she make her love known, and she will die if he woo her, rather than she will bate one breath of her accustomed crossness.

DON PEDRO.

She doth well: if she should make tender of her love, 'tis very possible he'll scorn it; for the man,—as you know all,—hath a contemptible spirit.

CLAUDIO.

He is a very proper man.

DON PEDRO.

He hath indeed a good outward happiness.

CLAUDIO.

'Fore God, and in my mind, very wise.

DON PEDRO.

He doth indeed show some sparks that are like wit.

CLAUDIO.

And I take him to be valiant.

DON PEDRO.

As Hector, I assure you: and in the managing of quarrels you may say he is wise; for either he avoids them with great discretion, or undertakes them with a most Christian-like fear.

LEONATO.

If he do fear God, a' must necessarily keep peace: if he break the peace, he ought to enter into a quarrel with fear and trembling.

DON PEDRO.

And so will he do; for the man doth fear God, howsoever it seems not in him by some large jests he will make. Well, I am sorry for your niece. Shall we go seek Benedick and tell him of her love?

CLAUDIO.

Never tell him, my lord: let her wear it out with good counsel.

LEONATO.

Nay, that's impossible: she may wear her heart out first.

DON PEDRO.

Well, we will hear further of it by your daughter: let it cool the while. I love Benedick well, and I could wish he would modestly examine himself, to see how much he is unworthy so good a lady.

LEONATO.

My lord, will you walk? dinner is ready.

CLAUDIO.

[Aside] If he do not dote on her upon this, I will never trust my expectation.

DON PEDRO.

[Aside] Let there be the same net spread for her; and that must your daughter and her gentlewoman carry. The sport will be, when they hold one an opinion of another's dotage, and no such matter: that's the scene that I would see, which will be merely a dumb show. Let us send her to call him in to dinner.

[Exeunt Don Pedro, Claudio and Leonato.]

BENEDICK.

[Advancing from the arbour.] This can be no trick: the conference was sadly borne. They have the truth of this from Hero. They seem to pity the lady: it seems her affections have their full bent. Love me? why, it must be requited. I hear how I am censured: they say I will bear myself proudly, if I perceive the love come from her; they say too that she will rather die than give any sign of affection. I did never think to marry: I must not seem proud: happy are they that hear their detractions, and can put them to mending. They say the lady is fair: 'tis a truth, I can bear them witness; and virtuous: 'tis so, I cannot reprove it; and wise, but for loving me: by my troth, it is no addition to her wit, nor no great argument of her folly, for I will be horribly in love with her. I may chance have some odd quirks and remnants of wit broken on me, because I have railed so long against marriage; but doth not the appetite alter? A man loves the meat in his youth that he cannot endure in his age. Shall quips and sentences and these paper bullets of the brain awe a man from the career of his humour? No; the world must be peopled. When I said I would die a bachelor, I did not think I should live till I were married. Here comes Beatrice. By this day! she's a fair lady: I do spy some marks of love in her.

Enter Beatrice.

BEATRICE.

Against my will I am sent to bid you come in to dinner.

BENEDICK.

Fair Beatrice, I thank you for your pains.

BEATRICE.

I took no more pains for those thanks than you take pains to thank me: if it had been painful, I would not have come.

BENEDICK.

You take pleasure then in the message?

BEATRICE.

Yea, just so much as you may take upon a knife's point, and choke a daw withal. You have no stomach, signior: fare you well.

[Exit.]

BENEDICK.

Ha! 'Against my will I am sent to bid you come in to dinner,' there's a double meaning in that. 'I took no more pains for those thanks than you took pains to thank me,' that's as much as to say, Any pains that I take for you is as easy as thanks. If I do not take pity of her, I am a villain; if I do not love her, I am a Jew. I will go get her picture.

[Exit.]

ACT III

SCENE I. Leonato's Garden.

Enter Hero, Margaret and Ursula.

HERO.

Good Margaret, run thee to the parlour;

There shalt thou find my cousin Beatrice

Proposing with the Prince and Claudio:

Whisper her ear, and tell her, I and Ursala

Walk in the orchard, and our whole discourse

Is all of her; say that thou overheard'st us,

And bid her steal into the pleached bower,

Where honey-suckles, ripen'd by the sun,

Forbid the sun to enter; like favourites,

Made proud by princes, that advance their pride

Against that power that bred it. There will she hide her,

To listen our propose. This is thy office;

Bear thee well in it and leave us alone.

MARGARET.

I'll make her come, I warrant you, presently.

[Exit.]

HERO.

Now, Ursula, when Beatrice doth come,

As we do trace this alley up and down,

Our talk must only be of Benedick:

When I do name him, let it be thy part

To praise him more than ever man did merit.

My talk to thee must be how Benedick

Is sick in love with Beatrice: of this matter

Is little Cupid's crafty arrow made,

That only wounds by hearsay.

Enter Beatrice behind.

Now begin;

For look where Beatrice, like a lapwing, runs

Close by the ground, to hear our conference.

URSULA.

The pleasant'st angling is to see the fish

Cut with her golden oars the silver stream,

And greedily devour the treacherous bait:

So angle we for Beatrice; who even now

Is couched in the woodbine coverture.

Fear you not my part of the dialogue.

HERO.

Then go we near her, that her ear lose nothing

Of the false sweet bait that we lay for it.

[They advance to the bower.]

No, truly, Ursula, she is too disdainful;

I know her spirits are as coy and wild

As haggards of the rock.

URSULA.

But are you sure

That Benedick loves Beatrice so entirely?

HERO.

So says the Prince, and my new-trothed lord.

URSULA.

And did they bid you tell her of it, madam?

HERO.

They did entreat me to acquaint her of it;

But I persuaded them, if they lov'd Benedick,

To wish him wrestle with affection,

And never to let Beatrice know of it.

URSULA.

Why did you so? Doth not the gentleman

Deserve as full as fortunate a bed

As ever Beatrice shall couch upon?

HERO.

O god of love! I know he doth deserve

As much as may be yielded to a man;

But Nature never fram'd a woman's heart

Of prouder stuff than that of Beatrice;

Disdain and scorn ride sparkling in her eyes,

Misprising what they look on, and her wit

Values itself so highly, that to her

All matter else seems weak. She cannot love,

Nor take no shape nor project of affection,

She is so self-endear'd.

URSULA.

Sure I think so;

And therefore certainly it were not good

She knew his love, lest she make sport at it.

HERO.

Why, you speak truth. I never yet saw man,

How wise, how noble, young, how rarely featur'd,

But she would spell him backward: if fair-fac'd,

She would swear the gentleman should be her sister;

If black, why, Nature, drawing of an antick,

Made a foul blot; if tall, a lance ill-headed;

If low, an agate very vilely cut;

If speaking, why, a vane blown with all winds;

If silent, why, a block moved with none.

180

So turns she every man the wrong side out,

And never gives to truth and virtue that

Which simpleness and merit purchaseth.

URSULA.

Sure, sure, such carping is not commendable.

HERO.

No; not to be so odd, and from all fashions,

As Beatrice is, cannot be commendable.

But who dare tell her so? If I should speak,

She would mock me into air: O! she would laugh me

Out of myself, press me to death with wit.

Therefore let Benedick, like cover'd fire,

Consume away in sighs, waste inwardly:

It were a better death than die with mocks,

Which is as bad as die with tickling.

URSULA.

Yet tell her of it: hear what she will say.

HERO.

No; rather I will go to Benedick,

And counsel him to fight against his passion.

And, truly, I'll devise some honest slanders

To stain my cousin with. One doth not know

How much an ill word may empoison liking.

URSULA.

O! do not do your cousin such a wrong.

She cannot be so much without true judgment,—

Having so swift and excellent a wit

As she is priz'd to have,—as to refuse

So rare a gentleman as Signior Benedick.

HERO.

He is the only man of Italy,

Always excepted my dear Claudio.

URSULA.

I pray you, be not angry with me, madam,

Speaking my fancy: Signior Benedick,

For shape, for bearing, argument and valour,

Goes foremost in report through Italy.

HERO.

Indeed, he hath an excellent good name.

URSULA.

His excellence did earn it, ere he had it.

When are you married, madam?

HERO.

Why, every day, tomorrow. Come, go in:

I'll show thee some attires, and have thy counsel

Which is the best to furnish me tomorrow.

URSULA.

She's lim'd, I warrant you,

We have caught her, madam.

HERO.

If it prove so, then loving goes by haps:

Some Cupid kills with arrows, some with traps.

[Exeunt Hero and Ursula.]

BEATRICE.

[Advancing.] What fire is in mine ears? Can this be true?

Stand I condemn'd for pride and scorn so much?

Contempt, farewell! and maiden pride, adieu!

No glory lives behind the back of such.

And, Benedick, love on; I will requite thee,

Taming my wild heart to thy loving hand:

If thou dost love, my kindness shall incite thee

To bind our loves up in a holy band;

For others say thou dost deserve, and I

Believe it better than reportingly.

[Exit.]

SCENE II. A Room in Leonato's House.

Enter Don Pedro, Claudio, Benedick and Leonato.

DON PEDRO.

I do but stay till your marriage be consummate, and then go I toward Arragon.

CLAUDIO.

I'll bring you thither, my lord, if you'll vouchsafe me.

DON PEDRO.

Nay, that would be as great a soil in the new gloss of your marriage, as to show a child his new coat and forbid him to wear it. I will only be bold with Benedick for his company; for, from the crown of his head to the sole of his foot, he is all mirth; he hath twice or thrice cut Cupid's bowstring, and the little hangman dare not shoot at him. He hath a heart as sound as a bell, and his tongue is the clapper; for what his heart thinks, his tongue speaks.

BENEDICK.

Gallants, I am not as I have been.

LEONATO.

So say I: methinks you are sadder.

CLAUDIO.

I hope he be in love.

DON PEDRO.

Hang him, truant! there's no true drop of blood in him to be truly touched with love. If he be sad, he wants money.

BENEDICK.

I have the tooth-ache.

DON PEDRO.

Draw it.

BENEDICK.

Hang it.

CLAUDIO.

You must hang it first, and draw it afterwards.

DON PEDRO.

What! sigh for the tooth-ache?

LEONATO.

Where is but a humour or a worm?

BENEDICK.

Well, everyone can master a grief but he that has it.

CLAUDIO.

Yet say I, he is in love.

DON PEDRO.

There is no appearance of fancy in him, unless it be a fancy that he hath to strange disguises; as to be a Dutchman today, a Frenchman tomorrow; or in the shape of two countries at once, as a German from the waist downward, all slops, and a Spaniard from the hip upward, no doublet. Unless he have a fancy to this foolery, as it appears he hath, he is no fool for fancy, as you would have it appear he is.

CLAUDIO.

If he be not in love with some woman, there is no believing old signs: a' brushes his hat a mornings; what should that bode?

DON PEDRO.

Hath any man seen him at the barber's?

CLAUDIO.

No, but the barber's man hath been seen with him; and the old ornament of his cheek hath already stuffed tennis balls.

LEONATO.

Indeed he looks younger than he did, by the loss of a beard.

DON PEDRO.

Nay, a' rubs himself with civet: can you smell him out by that?

CLAUDIO.

That's as much as to say the sweet youth's in love.

DON PEDRO.

The greatest note of it is his melancholy.

CLAUDIO.

And when was he wont to wash his face?

DON PEDRO.

Yea, or to paint himself? for the which, I hear what they say of him.

CLAUDIO.

Nay, but his jesting spirit; which is now crept into a lute-string, and now governed by stops.

DON PEDRO.

Indeed, that tells a heavy tale for him. Conclude, conclude he is in love.

CLAUDIO.

Nay, but I know who loves him.

DON PEDRO.

That would I know too: I warrant, one that knows him not.

CLAUDIO.

Yes, and his ill conditions; and in despite of all, dies for him.

DON PEDRO.

She shall be buried with her face upwards.

BENEDICK.

Yet is this no charm for the tooth-ache. Old signior, walk aside with me: I have studied eight or nine wise words to speak to you, which these hobby-horses must not hear.

[Exeunt Benedick and Leonato.]

DON PEDRO.

For my life, to break with him about Beatrice.

CLAUDIO.

'Tis even so. Hero and Margaret have by this played their parts with Beatrice, and then the two bears will not bite one another when they meet.

Enter Don John.

DON JOHN.

My lord and brother, God save you!

DON PEDRO.

Good den, brother.

DON JOHN.

If your leisure served, I would speak with you.

DON PEDRO.

In private?

DON JOHN.

If it please you; yet Count Claudio may hear, for what I would speak of concerns him.

DON PEDRO.

What's the matter?

DON JOHN.

[To Claudio.] Means your lordship to be married tomorrow?

DON PEDRO.

You know he does.

DON JOHN.

I know not that, when he knows what I know.

CLAUDIO.

If there be any impediment, I pray you discover it.

DON JOHN.

You may think I love you not: let that appear hereafter, and aim better at me by that I now will manifest. For my brother, I think he holds you well, and in dearness of heart hath holp to effect your ensuing marriage; surely suit ill-spent and labour ill bestowed!

DON PEDRO.

Why, what's the matter?

DON JOHN.

I came hither to tell you; and circumstances shortened,—for she has been too long a talking of,—the lady is disloyal.

CLAUDIO.

Who, Hero?

188

DON JOHN.

Even she: Leonato's Hero, your Hero, every man's Hero.

CLAUDIO.

Disloyal?

DON JOHN.

The word's too good to paint out her wickedness; I could say, she were worse: think you of a worse title, and I will fit her to it. Wonder not till further warrant: go but with me tonight, you shall see her chamber window entered, even the night before her wedding-day: if you love her then, tomorrow wed her; but it would better fit your honour to change your mind.

CLAUDIO.

May this be so?

DON PEDRO.

I will not think it.

DON JOHN.

If you dare not trust that you see, confess not that you know. If you will follow me, I will show you enough; and when you have seen more and heard more, proceed accordingly.

CLAUDIO.

If I see anything tonight why I should not marry her tomorrow, in the congregation, where I should wed, there will I shame her.

DON PEDRO.

And, as I wooed for thee to obtain her, I will join with thee to disgrace her.

DON JOHN.

I will disparage her no farther till you are my witnesses: bear it coldly but till midnight, and let the issue show itself.

DON PEDRO.

O day untowardly turned!

CLAUDIO.

O mischief strangely thwarting!

DON JOHN.

O plague right well prevented! So will you say when you have seen the sequel.

[Exeunt.]

Scene III. A Street.

Enter Dogberry and Verges, with the Watch.

DOGBERRY.

Are you good men and true?

VERGES.

Yea, or else it were pity but they should suffer salvation, body and soul.

DOGBERRY.

Nay, that were a punishment too good for them, if they should have any allegiance in them, being chosen for the Prince's watch.

VERGES.

Well, give them their charge, neighbour Dogberry.

DOGBERRY.

First, who think you the most desartless man to be constable?

FIRST WATCH.

Hugh Oatcake, sir, or George Seacoal; for they can write and read.

DOGBERRY.

Come hither, neighbour Seacoal. God hath blessed you with a good name: to be a well-favoured man is the gift of Fortune; but to write and read comes by Nature.

SECOND WATCH.

Both which, Master Constable,—

DOGBERRY.

You have: I knew it would be your answer. Well, for your favour, sir, why, give God thanks, and make no boast of it; and for your writing and reading, let that appear when there is no need of such vanity. You are thought here to be the most senseless and fit man for the constable of the watch; therefore bear you the lanthorn. This is your charge: you shall comprehend all vagrom men; you are to bid any man stand, in the Prince's name.

SECOND WATCH.

How, if a' will not stand?

DOGBERRY.

Why, then, take no note of him, but let him go; and presently call the rest of the watch together, and thank God you are rid of a knave.

VERGES.

If he will not stand when he is bidden, he is none of the Prince's subjects.

DOGBERRY.

True, and they are to meddle with none but the Prince's subjects. You shall also make no noise in the streets: for, for the watch to babble and to talk is most tolerable and not to be endured.

SECOND WATCH.

We will rather sleep than talk: we know what belongs to a watch.

DOGBERRY.

Why, you speak like an ancient and most quiet watchman, for I cannot see how sleeping should offend; only have a care that your bills be not stolen. Well, you are to call at all the alehouses, and bid those that are drunk get them to bed.

SECOND WATCH.

How if they will not?

DOGBERRY.

Why then, let them alone till they are sober: if they make you not then the better answer, you may say they are not the men you took them for.

SECOND WATCH.

Well, sir.

DOGBERRY.

If you meet a thief, you may suspect him, by virtue of your office, to be no true man; and, for such kind of men, the less you meddle or make with them, why, the more is for your honesty.

SECOND WATCH.

If we know him to be a thief, shall we not lay hands on him?

DOGBERRY.

Truly, by your office, you may; but I think they that touch pitch will be defiled. The most peaceable way for you, if you do take a thief, is to let him show himself what he is and steal out of your company.

VERGES.

You have been always called a merciful man, partner.

DOGBERRY.

Truly, I would not hang a dog by my will, much more a man who hath any honesty in him.

VERGES.

If you hear a child cry in the night, you must call to the nurse and bid her still it.

SECOND WATCH.

How if the nurse be asleep and will not hear us?

DOGBERRY.

Why then, depart in peace, and let the child wake her with crying; for the ewe that will not hear her lamb when it baes, will never answer a calf when he bleats.

VERGES.

'Tis very true.

DOGBERRY.

This is the end of the charge. You constable, are to present the Prince's own person: if you meet the Prince in the night, you may stay him.

VERGES.

Nay, by'r lady, that I think, a' cannot.

DOGBERRY.

Five shillings to one on't, with any man that knows the statutes, he may stay him: marry, not without the Prince be willing; for, indeed, the watch ought to offend no man, and it is an offence to stay a man against his will.

VERGES.

By'r lady, I think it be so.

DOGBERRY.

Ha, ah, ha! Well, masters, good night: an there be any matter of weight chances, call up me: keep your fellows' counsels and your own, and good night. Come, neighbour.

SECOND WATCH.

Well, masters, we hear our charge: let us go sit here upon the church bench till two, and then all to bed.

DOGBERRY.

One word more, honest neighbours. I pray you, watch about Signior Leonato's door; for the wedding being there tomorrow, there is a great coil tonight. Adieu; be vigitant, I beseech you.

[Exeunt Dogberry and Verges.]

Enter Borachio and Conrade.

BORACHIO.

What, Conrade!

WATCH.

[Aside] Peace! stir not.

BORACHIO.

Conrade, I say!

CONRADE.

Here, man. I am at thy elbow.

BORACHIO.

Mass, and my elbow itched; I thought there would a scab follow.

CONRADE.

I will owe thee an answer for that; and now forward with thy tale.

BORACHIO.

Stand thee close then under this penthouse, for it drizzles rain, and I will, like a true drunkard, utter all to thee.

WATCH.

[Aside] Some treason, masters; yet stand close.

BORACHIO.

Therefore know, I have earned of Don John a thousand ducats.

CONRADE.

Is it possible that any villainy should be so dear?

BORACHIO.

Thou shouldst rather ask if it were possible any villainy should be so rich; for when rich villains have need of poor ones, poor ones may make what price they will.

CONRADE.

I wonder at it.

BORACHIO.

That shows thou art unconfirmed. Thou knowest that the fashion of a doublet, or a hat, or a cloak, is nothing to a man.

CONRADE.

Yes, it is apparel.

BORACHIO.

I mean, the fashion.

CONRADE.

Yes, the fashion is the fashion.

BORACHIO.

Tush! I may as well say the fool's the fool. But seest thou not what a deformed thief this fashion is?

WATCH.

[Aside] I know that Deformed; a' has been a vile thief this seven years; a' goes up and down like a gentleman: I remember his name.

BORACHIO.

Didst thou not hear somebody?

CONRADE.

No: 'twas the vane on the house.

BORACHIO.

Seest thou not, I say, what a deformed thief this fashion is? how giddily he turns about all the hot bloods between fourteen and five-and-thirty? sometime fashioning them like Pharaoh's soldiers in the reechy painting; sometime like god Bel's priests in the old church window; sometime like the shaven Hercules in the smirched worm-eaten tapestry, where his codpiece seems as massy as his club?

CONRADE.

All this I see, and I see that the fashion wears out more apparel than the man. But art not thou thyself giddy with the fashion too, that thou hast shifted out of thy tale into telling me of the fashion?

BORACHIO.

Not so neither; but know, that I have tonight wooed Margaret, the Lady Hero's gentlewoman, by the name of Hero: she leans me out at her mistress' chamber window, bids me a thousand times good night,—I tell this tale vilely:—I should first tell thee how the Prince, Claudio, and my master, planted and placed and possessed by my master Don John, saw afar off in the orchard this amiable encounter.

CONRADE.

And thought they Margaret was Hero?

BORACHIO.

Two of them did, the Prince and Claudio; but the devil my master, knew she was Margaret; and partly by his oaths, which first possessed them, partly by the dark night, which did deceive them, but chiefly by my villainy, which did confirm any slander that Don John had made, away went Claudio enraged; swore he would meet her, as he was appointed, next morning at the temple, and there, before the whole congregation, shame her with what he saw o'er night, and send her home again without a husband.

FIRST WATCH.

We charge you in the Prince's name, stand!

SECOND WATCH.

Call up the right Master Constable. We have here recovered the most dangerous piece of lechery that ever was known in the commonwealth.

FIRST WATCH.

And one Deformed is one of them: I know him, a' wears a lock.

CONRADE.

Masters, masters!

SECOND WATCH.

You'll be made bring Deformed forth, I warrant you.

CONRADE.

Masters,—

FIRST WATCH.

Never speak: we charge you let us obey you to go with us.

BORACHIO. We are like to prove a goodly commodity, being taken up of these men's bills.

CONRADE.

A commodity in question, I warrant you. Come, we'll obey you.

[Exeunt.]

Scene IV. A Room in Leonato's House.

Enter Hero, Margaret and Ursula.

HERO.

Good Ursula, wake my cousin Beatrice, and desire her to rise.

URSULA.

I will, lady.

HERO.

And bid her come hither.

URSULA.

Well.

[Exit.]

MARGARET.

Troth, I think your other rebato were better.

HERO.

No, pray thee, good Meg, I'll wear this.

MARGARET.

By my troth's not so good; and I warrant your cousin will say so.

HERO.

My cousin 's a fool, and thou art another: I'll wear none but this.

MARGARET.

I like the new tire within excellently, if the hair were a thought browner; and your gown 's a most rare fashion, i' faith. I saw the Duchess of Milan's gown that they praise so.

HERO.

O! that exceeds, they say.

MARGARET.

By my troth 's but a night-gown in respect of yours: cloth o' gold, and cuts, and laced with silver, set with pearls, down sleeves, side sleeves, and skirts round, underborne with a bluish tinsel; but for a fine, quaint, graceful, and excellent fashion, yours is worth ten on't.

HERO.

God give me joy to wear it! for my heart is exceeding heavy.

MARGARET.

'Twill be heavier soon by the weight of a man.

HERO.

Fie upon thee! art not ashamed?

MARGARET.

Of what, lady? of speaking honourably? Is not marriage honourable in a beggar? Is not your lord honourable without marriage? I think you would have me say, saving your reverence, 'a husband:' an bad thinking do not wrest true speaking, I'll offend nobody. Is there any harm in 'the heavier for a husband'? None, I think, and it be the right husband and the right wife; otherwise 'tis light, and not heavy: ask my Lady Beatrice else; here she comes.

Enter Beatrice.

HERO.

Good morrow, coz.

BEATRICE.

Good morrow, sweet Hero.

HERO.

Why, how now? do you speak in the sick tune?

BEATRICE.

I am out of all other tune, methinks.

MARGARET.

Clap's into 'Light o' love'; that goes without a burden: do you sing it, and I'll dance it.

BEATRICE.

Ye, light o' love with your heels! then, if your husband have stables enough, you'll see he shall lack no barnes.

MARGARET.

O illegitimate construction! I scorn that with my heels.

BEATRICE.

'Tis almost five o'clock, cousin; 'tis time you were ready. By my troth, I am exceeding ill. Heigh-ho!

MARGARET.

For a hawk, a horse, or a husband?

BEATRICE.

For the letter that begins them all, H.

MARGARET.

Well, and you be not turned Turk, there's no more sailing by the star.

BEATRICE.

What means the fool, trow?

MARGARET.

Nothing I; but God send everyone their heart's desire!

HERO.

These gloves the Count sent me; they are an excellent perfume.

BEATRICE.

I am stuffed, cousin, I cannot smell.

MARGARET.

A maid, and stuffed! there's goodly catching of cold.

BEATRICE.

O, God help me! God help me! how long have you professed apprehension?

MARGARET.

Ever since you left it. Doth not my wit become me rarely!

BEATRICE.

It is not seen enough, you should wear it in your cap. By my troth, I am sick.

MARGARET.

Get you some of this distilled Carduus benedictus, and lay it to your heart: it is the only thing for a qualm.

HERO.

There thou prick'st her with a thistle.

BEATRICE.

Benedictus! why benedictus? you have some moral in this benedictus.

MARGARET.

Moral! no, by my troth, I have no moral meaning; I meant, plain holy thistle. You may think, perchance, that I think you are in love: nay, by'r Lady, I am not such a fool to think what I list; nor I list not to think what I can;

nor, indeed, I cannot think, if I would think my heart out of thinking, that you are in love, or that you will be in love, or that you can be in love. Yet Benedick was such another, and now is he become a man: he swore he would never marry; and yet now, in despite of his heart, he eats his meat without grudging: and how you may be converted, I know not; but methinks you look with your eyes as other women do.

BEATRICE.

What pace is this that thy tongue keeps?

MARGARET.

Not a false gallop.

Re-enter Ursula.

URSULA.

Madam, withdraw: the Prince, the Count, Signior Benedick, Don John, and all the gallants of the town are come to fetch you to church.

HERO.

Help to dress me, good coz, good Meg, good Ursula.

[Exeunt.]

Scene V. Another Room in Leonato's House.

Enter Leonato and Dogberry and Verges.

LEONATO.

What would you with me, honest neighbour?

DOGBERRY.

Marry, sir, I would have some confidence with you, that decerns you nearly.

LEONATO.

Brief, I pray you; for you see it is a busy time with me.

DOGBERRY.

Marry, this it is, sir.

VERGES.

Yes, in truth it is, sir.

LEONATO.

What is it, my good friends?

DOGBERRY.

Goodman Verges, sir, speaks a little off the matter: an old man, sir, and his wits are not so blunt as, God help, I would desire they were; but, in faith, honest as the skin between his brows.

VERGES.

Yes, I thank God, I am as honest as any man living, that is an old man and no honester than I.

DOGBERRY.

Comparisons are odorous: palabras, neighbour Verges.

LEONATO.

Neighbours, you are tedious.

DOGBERRY.

It pleases your worship to say so, but we are the poor Duke's officers; but truly, for mine own part, if I were as tedious as a king, I could find in my heart to bestow it all of your worship.

LEONATO.

All thy tediousness on me! ah?

DOGBERRY.

Yea, and 'twere a thousand pound more than 'tis; for I hear as good exclamation on your worship, as of any man in the city, and though I be but a poor man, I am glad to hear it.

VERGES.

And so am I.

LEONATO.

I would fain know what you have to say.

VERGES.

Marry, sir, our watch tonight, excepting your worship's presence, ha' ta'en a couple of as arrant knaves as any in Messina.

DOGBERRY.

A good old man, sir; he will be talking; as they say, 'when the age is in, the wit is out.' God help us! it is a world to see! Well said, i' faith, neighbour Verges: well, God's a good man; and two men ride of a horse, one must ride behind. An honest soul, i' faith, sir; by my troth he is, as ever broke bread; but God is to be worshipped: all men are not alike; alas! good neighbour.

LEONATO.

Indeed, neighbour, he comes too short of you.

DOGBERRY.

Gifts that God gives.

LEONATO.

I must leave you.

DOGBERRY.

One word, sir: our watch, sir, have indeed comprehended two aspicious persons, and we would have them this morning examined before your worship.

LEONATO.

Take their examination yourself, and bring it me: I am now in great haste, as may appear unto you.

DOGBERRY.

It shall be suffigance.

LEONATO.

Drink some wine ere you go: fare you well.

Enter a Messenger.

MESSENGER.

My lord, they stay for you to give your daughter to her husband.

LEONATO.

I'll wait upon them: I am ready.

[Exeunt Leonato and Messenger.]

DOGBERRY.

Go, good partner, go get you to Francis Seacoal; bid him bring his pen and inkhorn to the gaol: we are now to examination these men.

VERGES.

And we must do it wisely.

DOGBERRY.

We will spare for no wit, I warrant you; here's that shall drive some of them to a non-come: only get the learned writer to set down our excommunication, and meet me at the gaol.

[Exeunt.]

ACT IV

SCENE I. The Inside of a Church.

Enter Don Pedro, Don John, Leonato, Friar Francis, Claudio, Benedick, Hero, Beatrice &c.

LEONATO.

Come, Friar Francis, be brief: only to the plain form of marriage, and you shall recount their particular duties afterwards.

FRIAR.

You come hither, my lord, to marry this lady?

CLAUDIO.

No.

LEONATO.

To be married to her, friar; you come to marry her.

FRIAR.

Lady, you come hither to be married to this Count?

HERO.

I do.

FRIAR.

If either of you know any inward impediment, why you should not be conjoined, I charge you, on your souls, to utter it.

CLAUDIO.

Know you any, Hero?

HERO.

None, my lord.

FRIAR.

Know you any, Count?

LEONATO.

I dare make his answer; none.

CLAUDIO.

O! what men dare do! what men may do! what men daily do, not knowing what they do!

BENEDICK.

How now! Interjections? Why then, some be of laughing, as ah! ha! he!

CLAUDIO.

Stand thee by, Friar. Father, by your leave:

Will you with free and unconstrained soul

Give me this maid, your daughter?

LEONATO.

As freely, son, as God did give her me.

CLAUDIO.

And what have I to give you back whose worth

May counterpoise this rich and precious gift?

DON PEDRO.

Nothing, unless you render her again.

CLAUDIO.

Sweet Prince, you learn me noble thankfulness.

There, Leonato, take her back again:

Give not this rotten orange to your friend;

She's but the sign and semblance of her honour.

Behold! how like a maid she blushes here.

O! what authority and show of truth

Can cunning sin cover itself withal.

Comes not that blood as modest evidence

To witness simple virtue? Would you not swear,

All you that see her, that she were a maid,

By these exterior shows? But she is none:

She knows the heat of a luxurious bed;

Her blush is guiltiness, not modesty.

LEONATO.

What do you mean, my lord?

CLAUDIO.

Not to be married,

Not to knit my soul to an approved wanton.

LEONATO.

Dear my lord, if you, in your own proof,

Have vanquish'd the resistance of her youth,

And made defeat of her virginity,—

210

CLAUDIO.

I know what you would say: if I have known her,

You will say she did embrace me as a husband,

And so extenuate the forehand sin: No, Leonato,

I never tempted her with word too large;

But as a brother to his sister show'd

Bashful sincerity and comely love.

HERO.

And seem'd I ever otherwise to you?

CLAUDIO.

Out on thee! Seeming! I will write against it:

You seem to me as Dian in her orb,

As chaste as is the bud ere it be blown;

But you are more intemperate in your blood

Than Venus, or those pamper'd animals

That rage in savage sensuality.

HERO.

Is my lord well, that he doth speak so wide?

LEONATO.

Sweet Prince, why speak not you?

DON PEDRO.

What should I speak?

I stand dishonour'd, that have gone about

To link my dear friend to a common stale.

LEONATO.

Are these things spoken, or do I but dream?

DON JOHN.

Sir, they are spoken, and these things are true.

BENEDICK.

This looks not like a nuptial.

HERO.

True! O God!

CLAUDIO.

Leonato, stand I here?

Is this the Prince? Is this the Prince's brother?

Is this face Hero's? Are our eyes our own?

LEONATO.

All this is so; but what of this, my lord?

CLAUDIO.

Let me but move one question to your daughter,

And by that fatherly and kindly power

That you have in her, bid her answer truly.

LEONATO.

I charge thee do so, as thou art my child.

HERO.

O, God defend me! how am I beset!

What kind of catechizing call you this?

CLAUDIO.

To make you answer truly to your name.

HERO.

Is it not Hero? Who can blot that name

With any just reproach?

CLAUDIO.

Marry, that can Hero:

Hero itself can blot out Hero's virtue.

What man was he talk'd with you yesternight

Out at your window, betwixt twelve and one?

Now, if you are a maid, answer to this.

HERO.

I talk'd with no man at that hour, my lord.

DON PEDRO.

Why, then are you no maiden.

Leonato, I am sorry you must hear: upon my honour,

Myself, my brother, and this grieved Count,

Did see her, hear her, at that hour last night,

Talk with a ruffian at her chamber window;

Who hath indeed, most like a liberal villain,

Confess'd the vile encounters they have had

A thousand times in secret.

DON JOHN.

Fie, fie! they are not to be nam'd, my lord,

Not to be spoke of;

There is not chastity enough in language

Without offence to utter them. Thus, pretty lady,

I am sorry for thy much misgovernment.

CLAUDIO.

O Hero! what a Hero hadst thou been,

If half thy outward graces had been plac'd

About thy thoughts and counsels of thy heart!

But fare thee well, most foul, most fair! farewell,

Thou pure impiety, and impious purity!

For thee I'll lock up all the gates of love,

And on my eyelids shall conjecture hang,

To turn all beauty into thoughts of harm,

And never shall it more be gracious.

LEONATO.

Hath no man's dagger here a point for me?

[Hero swoons.]

BEATRICE.

Why, how now, cousin! wherefore sink you down?

DON JOHN.

Come, let us go. These things, come thus to light,

214

Smother her spirits up.

           [Exeunt Don Pedro, Don John and Claudio.]

BENEDICK.

How doth the lady?

BEATRICE.

Dead, I think! Help, uncle! Hero! why, Hero! Uncle! Signior Benedick! Friar!

LEONATO.

O Fate! take not away thy heavy hand:

Death is the fairest cover for her shame

That may be wish'd for.

BEATRICE.

How now, cousin Hero?

FRIAR.

Have comfort, lady.

LEONATO.

Dost thou look up?

FRIAR.

Yea; wherefore should she not?

LEONATO.

Wherefore! Why, doth not every earthly thing

Cry shame upon her? Could she here deny

The story that is printed in her blood?

Do not live, Hero; do not ope thine eyes;

For, did I think thou wouldst not quickly die,

Thought I thy spirits were stronger than thy shames,

Myself would, on the rearward of reproaches,

Strike at thy life. Griev'd I, I had but one?

Chid I for that at frugal Nature's frame?

O! one too much by thee. Why had I one?

Why ever wast thou lovely in my eyes?

Why had I not with charitable hand

Took up a beggar's issue at my gates,

Who smirched thus, and mir'd with infamy,

I might have said, 'No part of it is mine;

This shame derives itself from unknown loins?'

But mine, and mine I lov'd, and mine I prais'd,

And mine that I was proud on, mine so much

That I myself was to myself not mine,

Valuing of her; why, she—O! she is fallen

Into a pit of ink, that the wide sea

Hath drops too few to wash her clean again,

And salt too little which may season give

To her foul tainted flesh.

BENEDICK.

Sir, sir, be patient.

For my part, I am so attir'd in wonder,

I know not what to say.

BEATRICE.

O! on my soul, my cousin is belied!

BENEDICK.

Lady, were you her bedfellow last night?

BEATRICE.

No, truly, not; although, until last night,

I have this twelvemonth been her bedfellow.

LEONATO.

Confirm'd, confirm'd! O! that is stronger made,

Which was before barr'd up with ribs of iron.

Would the two princes lie? and Claudio lie,

Who lov'd her so, that, speaking of her foulness,

Wash'd it with tears? Hence from her! let her die.

FRIAR.

Hear me a little;

For I have only been silent so long,

And given way unto this course of fortune,

By noting of the lady: I have mark'd

A thousand blushing apparitions

To start into her face; a thousand innocent shames

In angel whiteness bear away those blushes;

And in her eye there hath appear'd a fire,

To burn the errors that these princes hold

Against her maiden truth. Call me a fool;

Trust not my reading nor my observations,

Which with experimental seal doth warrant

The tenure of my book; trust not my age,

My reverence, calling, nor divinity,

If this sweet lady lie not guiltless here

Under some biting error.

LEONATO.

Friar, it cannot be.

Thou seest that all the grace that she hath left

Is that she will not add to her damnation

A sin of perjury: she not denies it.

Why seek'st thou then to cover with excuse

That which appears in proper nakedness?

FRIAR.

Lady, what man is he you are accus'd of?

HERO.

They know that do accuse me, I know none;

If I know more of any man alive

Than that which maiden modesty doth warrant,

Let all my sins lack mercy! O, my father!

Prove you that any man with me convers'd

At hours unmeet, or that I yesternight

Maintain'd the change of words with any creature,

Refuse me, hate me, torture me to death.

FRIAR.

There is some strange misprision in the princes.

BENEDICK.

Two of them have the very bent of honour;

And if their wisdoms be misled in this,

The practice of it lives in John the bastard,

Whose spirits toil in frame of villainies.

LEONATO.

I know not. If they speak but truth of her,

These hands shall tear her; if they wrong her honour,

The proudest of them shall well hear of it.

Time hath not yet so dried this blood of mine,

Nor age so eat up my invention,

Nor fortune made such havoc of my means,

Nor my bad life reft me so much of friends,

But they shall find, awak'd in such a kind,

Both strength of limb and policy of mind,

Ability in means and choice of friends,

To quit me of them throughly.

FRIAR.

Pause awhile,

And let my counsel sway you in this case.

Your daughter here the princes left for dead;

Let her awhile be secretly kept in,

And publish it that she is dead indeed:

Maintain a mourning ostentation;

And on your family's old monument

Hang mournful epitaphs and do all rites

That appertain unto a burial.

LEONATO.

What shall become of this? What will this do?

FRIAR.

Marry, this well carried shall on her behalf

Change slander to remorse; that is some good.

But not for that dream I on this strange course,

But on this travail look for greater birth.

She dying, as it must be so maintain'd,

Upon the instant that she was accus'd,

Shall be lamented, pitied and excus'd

Of every hearer; for it so falls out

That what we have we prize not to the worth

Whiles we enjoy it, but being lack'd and lost,

Why, then we rack the value, then we find

The virtue that possession would not show us

Whiles it was ours. So will it fare with Claudio:

When he shall hear she died upon his words,

The idea of her life shall sweetly creep

Into his study of imagination,

And every lovely organ of her life

Shall come apparell'd in more precious habit,

More moving, delicate, and full of life

Into the eye and prospect of his soul,

Than when she liv'd indeed: then shall he mourn,—

If ever love had interest in his liver,—

And wish he had not so accused her,

No, though he thought his accusation true.

Let this be so, and doubt not but success

Will fashion the event in better shape

Than I can lay it down in likelihood.

But if all aim but this be levell'd false,

The supposition of the lady's death

Will quench the wonder of her infamy:

And if it sort not well, you may conceal her,—

As best befits her wounded reputation,—

In some reclusive and religious life,

Out of all eyes, tongues, minds, and injuries.

BENEDICK.

Signior Leonato, let the friar advise you:

And though you know my inwardness and love

Is very much unto the Prince and Claudio,

Yet, by mine honour, I will deal in this

As secretly and justly as your soul

Should with your body.

LEONATO.

Being that I flow in grief,

The smallest twine may lead me.

FRIAR.

'Tis well consented: presently away;

For to strange sores strangely they strain the cure.

Come, lady, die to live: this wedding day

Perhaps is but prolong'd: have patience and endure.

[Exeunt Friar, Hero and Leonato.]

BENEDICK.

Lady Beatrice, have you wept all this while?

BEATRICE.

Yea, and I will weep a while longer.

BENEDICK.

I will not desire that.

BEATRICE.

You have no reason; I do it freely.

BENEDICK.

Surely I do believe your fair cousin is wronged.

BEATRICE.

Ah! how much might the man deserve of me that would right her.

BENEDICK.

Is there any way to show such friendship?

BEATRICE.

A very even way, but no such friend.

BENEDICK.

May a man do it?

BEATRICE.

It is a man's office, but not yours.

BENEDICK.

I do love nothing in the world so well as you: is not that strange?

BEATRICE.

As strange as the thing I know not. It were as possible for me to say I loved nothing so well as you; but believe me not, and yet I lie not; I confess nothing, nor I deny nothing. I am sorry for my cousin.

BENEDICK.

By my sword, Beatrice, thou lovest me.

BEATRICE.

Do not swear by it, and eat it.

BENEDICK.

I will swear by it that you love me; and I will make him eat it that says I love not you.

BEATRICE.

Will you not eat your word?

BENEDICK.

With no sauce that can be devised to it. I protest I love thee.

BEATRICE.

Why then, God forgive me!

BENEDICK.

What offence, sweet Beatrice?

BEATRICE.

You have stayed me in a happy hour: I was about to protest I loved you.

BENEDICK.

And do it with all thy heart.

BEATRICE.

I love you with so much of my heart that none is left to protest.

BENEDICK.

Come, bid me do anything for thee.

BEATRICE.

Kill Claudio.

BENEDICK.

Ha! not for the wide world.

BEATRICE.

You kill me to deny it. Farewell.

BENEDICK.

Tarry, sweet Beatrice.

BEATRICE.

I am gone, though I am here: there is no love in you: nay, I pray you, let me go.

BENEDICK.

Beatrice,—

BEATRICE.

In faith, I will go.

BENEDICK.

We'll be friends first.

BEATRICE.

You dare easier be friends with me than fight with mine enemy.

BENEDICK.

Is Claudio thine enemy?

BEATRICE.

Is he not approved in the height a villain, that hath slandered, scorned, dishonoured my kinswoman? O! that I were a man. What! bear her in hand until they come to take hands, and then, with public accusation, uncovered slander, unmitigated rancour,—O God, that I were a man! I would eat his heart in the market-place.

BENEDICK.

Hear me, Beatrice,—

BEATRICE.

Talk with a man out at a window! a proper saying!

BENEDICK.

Nay, but Beatrice,—

BEATRICE.

Sweet Hero! she is wronged, she is slandered, she is undone.

BENEDICK.

Beat—

BEATRICE.

Princes and Counties! Surely, a princely testimony, a goodly Count Comfect; a sweet gallant, surely! O! that I were a man for his sake, or that I had any friend would be a man for my sake! But manhood is melted into curtsies, valour into compliment, and men are only turned into tongue, and trim ones too: he is now as valiant as Hercules, that only tells a lie and swears it. I cannot be a man with wishing, therefore I will die a woman with grieving.

BENEDICK.

Tarry, good Beatrice. By this hand, I love thee.

BEATRICE.

Use it for my love some other way than swearing by it.

BENEDICK.

Think you in your soul the Count Claudio hath wronged Hero?

BEATRICE.

Yea, as sure is I have a thought or a soul.

BENEDICK.

Enough! I am engaged, I will challenge him. I will kiss your hand, and so leave you. By this hand, Claudio shall render me a dear account. As you hear of me, so think of me. Go, comfort your cousin: I must say she is dead; and so, farewell.

[Exeunt.]

Scene II. A Prison.

Enter Dogberry, Verges, and Sexton, in gowns; and the Watch, with Conrade and Borachio.

DOGBERRY.

Is our whole dissembly appeared?

VERGES.

O! a stool and a cushion for the sexton.

SEXTON.

Which be the malefactors?

DOGBERRY.

Marry, that am I and my partner.

VERGES.

Nay, that's certain: we have the exhibition to examine.

SEXTON.

But which are the offenders that are to be examined? let them come before Master Constable.

DOGBERRY.

Yea, marry, let them come before me. What is your name, friend?

BORACHIO.

Borachio.

DOGBERRY.

Pray write down Borachio. Yours, sirrah?

CONRADE.

I am a gentleman, sir, and my name is Conrade.

DOGBERRY.

Write down Master gentleman Conrade. Masters, do you serve God?

BOTH.

Yea, sir, we hope.

DOGBERRY.

Write down that they hope they serve God: and write God first; for God defend but God should go before such villains! Masters, it is proved already that you are little better than false knaves, and it will go near to be thought so shortly. How answer you for yourselves?

CONRADE.

Marry, sir, we say we are none.

DOGBERRY.

A marvellous witty fellow, I assure you; but I will go about with him. Come you hither, sirrah; a word in your ear: sir, I say to you, it is thought you are false knaves.

BORACHIO.

Sir, I say to you we are none.

DOGBERRY.

Well, stand aside. Fore God, they are both in a tale. Have you writ down, that they are none?

SEXTON.

Master Constable, you go not the way to examine: you must call forth the watch that are their accusers.

DOGBERRY.

Yea, marry, that's the eftest way. Let the watch come forth. Masters, I charge you, in the Prince's name, accuse these men.

FIRST WATCH.

This man said, sir, that Don John, the Prince's brother, was a villain.

DOGBERRY.

Write down Prince John a villain. Why, this is flat perjury, to call a Prince's brother villain.

BORACHIO.

Master Constable,—

DOGBERRY.

Pray thee, fellow, peace: I do not like thy look, I promise thee.

SEXTON.

What heard you him say else?

SECOND WATCH.

Marry, that he had received a thousand ducats of Don John for accusing the Lady Hero wrongfully.

DOGBERRY.

Flat burglary as ever was committed.

VERGES.

Yea, by the mass, that it is.

SEXTON.

What else, fellow?

FIRST WATCH.

And that Count Claudio did mean, upon his words, to disgrace Hero before the whole assembly, and not marry her.

DOGBERRY.

O villain! thou wilt be condemned into everlasting redemption for this.

SEXTON.

What else?

SECOND WATCH.

This is all.

SEXTON.

And this is more, masters, than you can deny. Prince John is this morning secretly stolen away: Hero was in this manner accused, in this manner refused, and, upon the grief of this, suddenly died. Master Constable, let these men be bound, and brought to Leonato's: I will go before and show him their examination.

[Exit.]

DOGBERRY.

Come, let them be opinioned.

VERGES.

Let them be in the hands—

CONRADE.

Off, coxcomb!

DOGBERRY.

God's my life! where's the sexton? let him write down the Prince's officer coxcomb. Come, bind them. Thou naughty varlet!

CONRADE.

Away! you are an ass; you are an ass.

DOGBERRY.

Dost thou not suspect my place? Dost thou not suspect my years? O that he were here to write me down an ass! but, masters, remember that I am an ass; though it be not written down, yet forget not that I am an ass. No, thou villain, thou art full of piety, as shall be proved upon thee by good witness. I am a wise fellow; and, which is more, an officer; and, which is more, a householder; and, which is more, as pretty a piece of flesh as any in Messina; and one that knows the law, go to; and a rich fellow enough, go to; and a fellow that hath had losses; and one that hath two gowns, and everything handsome about him. Bring him away. O that I had been writ down an ass!

[Exeunt.]

ACT V

SCENE I. Before Leonato's House.

Enter Leonato and Antonio.

ANTONIO.

If you go on thus, you will kill yourself

And 'tis not wisdom thus to second grief

Against yourself.

LEONATO.

I pray thee, cease thy counsel,

Which falls into mine ears as profitless

As water in a sieve: give not me counsel;

Nor let no comforter delight mine ear

But such a one whose wrongs do suit with mine:

Bring me a father that so lov'd his child,

Whose joy of her is overwhelm'd like mine,

And bid him speak of patience;

Measure his woe the length and breadth of mine,

And let it answer every strain for strain,

As thus for thus and such a grief for such,

In every lineament, branch, shape, and form:

If such a one will smile, and stroke his beard;

Bid sorrow wag, cry 'hem' when he should groan,

Patch grief with proverbs; make misfortune drunk

With candle-wasters; bring him yet to me,

And I of him will gather patience.

But there is no such man; for, brother, men

Can counsel and speak comfort to that grief

Which they themselves not feel; but, tasting it,

Their counsel turns to passion, which before

Would give preceptial medicine to rage,

Fetter strong madness in a silken thread,

Charm ache with air and agony with words.

No, no; 'tis all men's office to speak patience

To those that wring under the load of sorrow,

But no man's virtue nor sufficiency

To be so moral when he shall endure

The like himself. Therefore give me no counsel:

My griefs cry louder than advertisement.

ANTONIO.

Therein do men from children nothing differ.

LEONATO.

I pray thee peace! I will be flesh and blood;

For there was never yet philosopher

That could endure the toothache patiently,

However they have writ the style of gods

And made a push at chance and sufferance.

ANTONIO.

Yet bend not all the harm upon yourself;

Make those that do offend you suffer too.

LEONATO.

There thou speak'st reason: nay, I will do so.

My soul doth tell me Hero is belied;

And that shall Claudio know; so shall the Prince,

And all of them that thus dishonour her.

ANTONIO.

Here comes the Prince and Claudio hastily.

Enter Don Pedro and Claudio.

DON PEDRO.

Good den, good den.

CLAUDIO.

Good day to both of you.

LEONATO.

Hear you, my lords,—

DON PEDRO.

We have some haste, Leonato.

LEONATO.

Some haste, my lord! well, fare you well, my lord:

Are you so hasty now?—well, all is one.

DON PEDRO.

Nay, do not quarrel with us, good old man.

ANTONIO.

If he could right himself with quarrelling,

Some of us would lie low.

CLAUDIO.

Who wrongs him?

LEONATO.

Marry, thou dost wrong me; thou dissembler, thou.

Nay, never lay thy hand upon thy sword;

I fear thee not.

CLAUDIO.

Marry, beshrew my hand,

If it should give your age such cause of fear.

In faith, my hand meant nothing to my sword.

LEONATO.

Tush, tush, man! never fleer and jest at me:

I speak not like a dotard nor a fool,

As, under privilege of age, to brag

What I have done being young, or what would do,

Were I not old. Know, Claudio, to thy head,

Thou hast so wrong'd mine innocent child and me

That I am forc'd to lay my reverence by,

And, with grey hairs and bruise of many days,

Do challenge thee to trial of a man.

I say thou hast belied mine innocent child:

Thy slander hath gone through and through her heart,

And she lies buried with her ancestors;

O! in a tomb where never scandal slept,

Save this of hers, fram'd by thy villainy!

CLAUDIO.

My villainy?

LEONATO.

Thine, Claudio; thine, I say.

DON PEDRO.

You say not right, old man,

LEONATO.

My lord, my lord,

I'll prove it on his body, if he dare,

Despite his nice fence and his active practice,

His May of youth and bloom of lustihood.

CLAUDIO.

Away! I will not have to do with you.

LEONATO.

Canst thou so daff me? Thou hast kill'd my child;

If thou kill'st me, boy, thou shalt kill a man.

ANTONIO.

He shall kill two of us, and men indeed:

But that's no matter; let him kill one first:

Win me and wear me; let him answer me.

Come, follow me, boy; come, sir boy, come, follow me.

Sir boy, I'll whip you from your foining fence;

Nay, as I am a gentleman, I will.

LEONATO.

Brother,—

ANTONIO.

Content yourself. God knows I lov'd my niece;

And she is dead, slander'd to death by villains,

That dare as well answer a man indeed

As I dare take a serpent by the tongue.

Boys, apes, braggarts, Jacks, milksops!

LEONATO.

Brother Anthony,—

ANTONIO.

Hold you content. What, man! I know them, yea,

And what they weigh, even to the utmost scruple,

Scambling, out-facing, fashion-monging boys,

That lie and cog and flout, deprave and slander,

Go antickly, show outward hideousness,

And speak off half a dozen dangerous words,

How they might hurt their enemies, if they durst;

And this is all!

LEONATO.

But, brother Anthony,—

ANTONIO.

Come, 'tis no matter:

Do not you meddle, let me deal in this.

DON PEDRO.

Gentlemen both, we will not wake your patience.

My heart is sorry for your daughter's death;

But, on my honour, she was charg'd with nothing

But what was true and very full of proof.

LEONATO.

My lord, my lord—

DON PEDRO.

I will not hear you.

LEONATO.

No? Come, brother, away. I will be heard.—

ANTONIO.

And shall, or some of us will smart for it.

[Exeunt Leonato and Antonio.]

Enter Benedick.

DON PEDRO.

See, see; here comes the man we went to seek.

CLAUDIO.

Now, signior, what news?

BENEDICK.

Good day, my lord.

DON PEDRO.

Welcome, signior: you are almost come to part almost a fray.

CLAUDIO.

We had like to have had our two noses snapped off with two old men without teeth.

DON PEDRO.

Leonato and his brother. What think'st thou? Had we fought, I doubt we should have been too young for them.

BENEDICK.

In a false quarrel there is no true valour. I came to seek you both.

CLAUDIO.

We have been up and down to seek thee; for we are high-proof melancholy, and would fain have it beaten away. Wilt thou use thy wit?

BENEDICK.

It is in my scabbard; shall I draw it?

DON PEDRO.

Dost thou wear thy wit by thy side?

CLAUDIO.

Never any did so, though very many have been beside their wit. I will bid thee draw, as we do the minstrels; draw, to pleasure us.

DON PEDRO.

As I am an honest man, he looks pale. Art thou sick, or angry?

CLAUDIO.

What, courage, man! What though care killed a cat, thou hast mettle enough in thee to kill care.

BENEDICK.

Sir, I shall meet your wit in the career, and you charge it against me. I pray you choose another subject.

CLAUDIO.

Nay then, give him another staff: this last was broke cross.

DON PEDRO.

By this light, he changes more and more: I think he be angry indeed.

CLAUDIO.

If he be, he knows how to turn his girdle.

BENEDICK.

Shall I speak a word in your ear?

CLAUDIO.

God bless me from a challenge!

BENEDICK.

[Aside to Claudio.] You are a villain, I jest not: I will make it good how you dare, with what you dare, and when you dare. Do me right, or I will protest your cowardice. You have killed a sweet lady, and her death shall fall heavy on you. Let me hear from you.

CLAUDIO.

Well I will meet you, so I may have good cheer.

DON PEDRO.

What, a feast, a feast?

CLAUDIO.

I' faith, I thank him; he hath bid me to a calf's-head and a capon, the which if I do not carve most curiously, say my knife's naught. Shall I not find a woodcock too?

BENEDICK.

Sir, your wit ambles well; it goes easily.

DON PEDRO.

I'll tell thee how Beatrice praised thy wit the other day. I said, thou hadst a fine wit. 'True,' says she, 'a fine little one.' 'No,' said I, 'a great wit.' 'Right,' said she, 'a great gross one.' 'Nay,' said I, 'a good wit.' 'Just,' said she, 'it hurts nobody.' 'Nay,' said I, 'the gentleman is wise.' 'Certain,' said she, 'a wise gentleman.' 'Nay,' said I, 'he hath the tongues.' 'That I believe' said she, 'for he swore a thing to me on Monday night, which he forswore on Tuesday morning: there's a double tongue; there's two tongues.' Thus did she, an hour together, trans-shape thy particular virtues; yet at last she concluded with a sigh, thou wast the properest man in Italy.

CLAUDIO.

For the which she wept heartily and said she cared not.

DON PEDRO.

Yea, that she did; but yet, for all that, an if she did not hate him deadly, she would love him dearly. The old man's daughter told us all.

CLAUDIO.

All, all; and moreover, God saw him when he was hid in the garden.

DON PEDRO.

But when shall we set the savage bull's horns on the sensible Benedick's head?

CLAUDIO.

Yea, and text underneath, 'Here dwells Benedick the married man!'

BENEDICK.

Fare you well, boy: you know my mind. I will leave you now to your gossip-like humour; you break jests as braggarts do their blades, which, God be thanked, hurt not. My lord, for your many courtesies I thank you: I must discontinue your company. Your brother the bastard is fled from Messina: you have, among you, killed a sweet and innocent lady. For my Lord Lackbeard there, he and I shall meet; and till then, peace be with him.

[Exit.]

DON PEDRO.

He is in earnest.

CLAUDIO.

In most profound earnest; and, I'll warrant you, for the love of Beatrice.

DON PEDRO.

And hath challenged thee?

CLAUDIO.

Most sincerely.

DON PEDRO.

What a pretty thing man is when he goes in his doublet and hose and leaves off his wit!

CLAUDIO.

He is then a giant to an ape; but then is an ape a doctor to such a man.

DON PEDRO.

But, soft you; let me be: pluck up, my heart, and be sad! Did he not say my brother was fled?

Enter Dogberry, Verges, and the Watch, with Conrade and Borachio.

DOGBERRY.

Come you, sir: if justice cannot tame you, she shall ne'er weigh more reasons in her balance. Nay, an you be a cursing hypocrite once, you must be looked to.

DON PEDRO.

How now! two of my brother's men bound! Borachio, one!

CLAUDIO.

Hearken after their offence, my lord.

DON PEDRO.

Officers, what offence have these men done?

DOGBERRY.

Marry, sir, they have committed false report; moreover, they have spoken untruths; secondarily, they are slanders; sixth and lastly, they have belied a lady; thirdly, they have verified unjust things; and to conclude, they are lying knaves.

DON PEDRO.

First, I ask thee what they have done; thirdly, I ask thee what's their offence; sixth and lastly, why they are committed; and, to conclude, what you

244

lay to their charge?

CLAUDIO.

Rightly reasoned, and in his own division; and, by my troth, there's one meaning well suited.

DON PEDRO.

Who have you offended, masters, that you are thus bound to your answer? This learned constable is too cunning to be understood. What's your offence?

BORACHIO.

Sweet Prince, let me go no farther to mine answer: do you hear me, and let this Count kill me. I have deceived even your very eyes: what your wisdoms could not discover, these shallow fools have brought to light; who, in the night overheard me confessing to this man how Don John your brother incensed me to slander the Lady Hero; how you were brought into the orchard and saw me court Margaret in Hero's garments; how you disgraced her, when you should marry her. My villainy they have upon record; which I had rather seal with my death than repeat over to my shame. The lady is dead upon mine and my master's false accusation; and, briefly, I desire nothing but the reward of a villain.

DON PEDRO.

Runs not this speech like iron through your blood?

CLAUDIO.

I have drunk poison whiles he utter'd it.

DON PEDRO.

But did my brother set thee on to this?

BORACHIO.

Yea; and paid me richly for the practice of it.

DON PEDRO.

He is compos'd and fram'd of treachery: And fled he is upon this villainy.

CLAUDIO.

Sweet Hero! now thy image doth appear

In the rare semblance that I lov'd it first.

DOGBERRY.

Come, bring away the plaintiffs: by this time our sexton hath reformed Signior Leonato of the matter. And masters, do not forget to specify, when time and place shall serve, that I am an ass.

VERGES.

Here, here comes Master Signior Leonato, and the sexton too.

Re-enter Leonato, Antonio and the Sexton.

LEONATO.

Which is the villain? Let me see his eyes,

That, when I note another man like him,

I may avoid him. Which of these is he?

BORACHIO.

If you would know your wronger, look on me.

LEONATO.

Art thou the slave that with thy breath hast kill'd

Mine innocent child?

BORACHIO.

Yea, even I alone.

LEONATO.

No, not so, villain; thou beliest thyself:

Here stand a pair of honourable men;

A third is fled, that had a hand in it.

I thank you, princes, for my daughter's death:

Record it with your high and worthy deeds.

'Twas bravely done, if you bethink you of it.

CLAUDIO.

I know not how to pray your patience;

Yet I must speak. Choose your revenge yourself;

Impose me to what penance your invention

Can lay upon my sin: yet sinn'd I not

But in mistaking.

DON PEDRO.

By my soul, nor I:

And yet, to satisfy this good old man,

I would bend under any heavy weight

That he'll enjoin me to.

LEONATO.

I cannot bid you bid my daughter live;

That were impossible; but, I pray you both,

Possess the people in Messina here

How innocent she died; and if your love

Can labour aught in sad invention,

Hang her an epitaph upon her tomb,

And sing it to her bones: sing it tonight.

Tomorrow morning come you to my house,

And since you could not be my son-in-law,

Be yet my nephew. My brother hath a daughter,

Almost the copy of my child that's dead,

And she alone is heir to both of us:

Give her the right you should have given her cousin,

And so dies my revenge.

CLAUDIO.

O noble sir,

Your over-kindness doth wring tears from me!

I do embrace your offer; and dispose

For henceforth of poor Claudio.

LEONATO.

Tomorrow then I will expect your coming;

Tonight I take my leave. This naughty man

Shall face to face be brought to Margaret,

Who, I believe, was pack'd in all this wrong,

Hir'd to it by your brother.

BORACHIO.

No, by my soul she was not;

Nor knew not what she did when she spoke to me;

But always hath been just and virtuous

In anything that I do know by her.

DOGBERRY.

Moreover, sir,—which, indeed, is not under white and black,— this plaintiff here, the offender, did call me ass: I beseech you, let it be remembered in his punishment. And also, the watch heard them talk of one Deformed: they say he wears a key in his ear and a lock hanging by it, and borrows money in God's name, the which he hath used so long and never paid, that now men grow hard-hearted, and will lend nothing for God's sake. Pray you, examine him upon that point.

LEONATO.

I thank thee for thy care and honest pains.

DOGBERRY.

Your worship speaks like a most thankful and reverent youth, and I praise God for you.

LEONATO.

There's for thy pains.

DOGBERRY.

God save the foundation!

LEONATO.

Go, I discharge thee of thy prisoner, and I thank thee.

DOGBERRY.

I leave an arrant knave with your worship; which I beseech your worship to correct yourself, for the example of others. God keep your worship! I wish your worship well; God restore you to health! I humbly give you leave to depart, and if a merry meeting may be wished, God prohibit it! Come, neighbour.

[Exeunt Dogberry and Verges.]

LEONATO.

Until tomorrow morning, lords, farewell.

ANTONIO.

Farewell, my lords: we look for you tomorrow.

DON PEDRO.

We will not fail.

CLAUDIO.

Tonight I'll mourn with Hero.

[Exeunt Don Pedro and Claudio.]

LEONATO.

[To the Watch.] Bring you these fellows on. We'll talk with Margaret,

How her acquaintance grew with this lewd fellow.

[Exeunt.]

SCENE II. Leonato's Garden.

Enter Benedick and Margaret, meeting.

BENEDICK.

Pray thee, sweet Mistress Margaret, deserve well at my hands by helping me to the speech of Beatrice.

MARGARET.

Will you then write me a sonnet in praise of my beauty?

BENEDICK.

In so high a style, Margaret, that no man living shall come over it; for, in most comely truth, thou deservest it.

MARGARET.

To have no man come over me! why, shall I always keep below stairs?

BENEDICK.

Thy wit is as quick as the greyhound's mouth; it catches.

MARGARET.

And yours as blunt as the fencer's foils, which hit, but hurt not.

BENEDICK.

A most manly wit, Margaret; it will not hurt a woman: and so, I pray thee, call Beatrice. I give thee the bucklers.

MARGARET.

Give us the swords, we have bucklers of our own.

BENEDICK.

If you use them, Margaret, you must put in the pikes with a vice; and they are dangerous weapons for maids.

MARGARET.

Well, I will call Beatrice to you, who I think hath legs.

BENEDICK.

And therefore will come.

[Exit Margaret.]

The god of love,

That sits above,

And knows me, and knows me,

How pitiful I deserve,—

I mean, in singing: but in loving, Leander the good swimmer, Troilus the first employer of panders, and a whole book full of these quondam carpet-mongers, whose names yet run smoothly in the even road of a blank verse, why, they were never so truly turned over and over as my poor self in love. Marry, I cannot show it in rime; I have tried: I can find out no rime to 'lady' but 'baby', an innocent rime; for 'scorn,' 'horn', a hard rime; for 'school', 'fool', a babbling rime; very ominous endings: no, I was not born under a riming planet, nor I cannot woo in festival terms.

Enter Beatrice.

Sweet Beatrice, wouldst thou come when I called thee?

BEATRICE.

Yea, signior; and depart when you bid me.

BENEDICK.

O, stay but till then!

BEATRICE.

'Then' is spoken; fare you well now: and yet, ere I go, let me go with that I came for; which is, with knowing what hath passed between you and Claudio.

BENEDICK.

Only foul words; and thereupon I will kiss thee.

BEATRICE.

Foul words is but foul wind, and foul wind is but foul breath, and foul breath is noisome; therefore I will depart unkissed.

BENEDICK.

Thou hast frighted the word out of his right sense, so forcible is thy wit. But I must tell thee plainly, Claudio undergoes my challenge, and either I must shortly hear from him, or I will subscribe him a coward. And, I pray thee now, tell me, for which of my bad parts didst thou first fall in love with me?

BEATRICE.

For them all together; which maintained so politic a state of evil that they will not admit any good part to intermingle with them. But for which of my good parts did you first suffer love for me?

BENEDICK.

'Suffer love,' a good epithet! I do suffer love indeed, for I love thee against my will.

BEATRICE.

In spite of your heart, I think. Alas, poor heart! If you spite it for my sake, I will spite it for yours; for I will never love that which my friend hates.

BENEDICK.

Thou and I are too wise to woo peaceably.

BEATRICE.

It appears not in this confession: there's not one wise man among twenty that will praise himself.

BENEDICK.

An old, an old instance, Beatrice, that lived in the time of good neighbours. If a man do not erect in this age his own tomb ere he dies, he shall live no longer in monument than the bell rings and the widow weeps.

BEATRICE.

And how long is that think you?

BENEDICK.

Question: why, an hour in clamour and a quarter in rheum: therefore is it most expedient for the wise,—if Don Worm, his conscience, find no impediment to the contrary,—to be the trumpet of his own virtues, as I am to myself. So much for praising myself, who, I myself will bear witness, is praiseworthy. And now tell me, how doth your cousin?

BEATRICE.

Very ill.

BENEDICK.

And how do you?

BEATRICE.

Very ill too.

BENEDICK.

Serve God, love me, and mend. There will I leave you too, for here comes one in haste.

Enter Ursula.

URSULA.

Madam, you must come to your uncle. Yonder's old coil at home: it is proved, my Lady Hero hath been falsely accused, the Prince and Claudio mightily abused; and Don John is the author of all, who is fled and gone. Will you come presently?

BEATRICE.

Will you go hear this news, signior?

BENEDICK.

I will live in thy heart, die in thy lap, and be buried in thy eyes; and moreover I will go with thee to thy uncle's.

[Exeunt.]

SCENE III. The Inside of a Church.

Enter Don Pedro, Claudio and Attendants, with music and tapers.

CLAUDIO.

Is this the monument of Leonato?

A LORD.

It is, my lord.

CLAUDIO.

[Reads from a scroll.]

Epitaph.

Done to death by slanderous tongues

  Was the Hero that here lies:

Death, in guerdon of her wrongs,

  Gives her fame which never dies.

So the life that died with shame

  Lives in death with glorious fame.

Hang thou there upon the tomb,

Praising her when I am dumb.

Now, music, sound, and sing your solemn hymn.

Song.

Pardon, goddess of the night,

  Those that slew thy virgin knight;

  For the which, with songs of woe,

  Round about her tomb they go.

Midnight, assist our moan;

Help us to sigh and groan,

   Heavily, heavily:

Graves, yawn and yield your dead,

Till death be uttered,

   Heavily, heavily.

CLAUDIO.

Now, unto thy bones good night!

Yearly will I do this rite.

DON PEDRO.

Good morrow, masters: put your torches out.

The wolves have prey'd; and look, the gentle day,

Before the wheels of Phoebus, round about

Dapples the drowsy East with spots of grey.

Thanks to you all, and leave us: fare you well.

CLAUDIO.

Good morrow, masters: each his several way.

DON PEDRO.

Come, let us hence, and put on other weeds;

And then to Leonato's we will go.

CLAUDIO.

And Hymen now with luckier issue speed's,

Than this for whom we rend'red up this woe!

[Exeunt.]

SCENE IV. A Room in Leonato's House.

Enter Leonato, Antonio, Benedick, Beatrice, Margaret, Ursula, Friar Francis and Hero.

FRIAR.

Did I not tell you she was innocent?

LEONATO.

So are the Prince and Claudio, who accus'd her

Upon the error that you heard debated:

But Margaret was in some fault for this,

Although against her will, as it appears

In the true course of all the question.

ANTONIO.

Well, I am glad that all things sort so well.

BENEDICK.

And so am I, being else by faith enforc'd

To call young Claudio to a reckoning for it.

LEONATO.

Well, daughter, and you gentlewomen all,

Withdraw into a chamber by yourselves,

And when I send for you, come hither mask'd:

The Prince and Claudio promis'd by this hour

To visit me.

[Exeunt Ladies.]

You know your office, brother;

You must be father to your brother's daughter,

And give her to young Claudio.

ANTONIO.

Which I will do with confirm'd countenance.

BENEDICK.

Friar, I must entreat your pains, I think.

FRIAR.

To do what, signior?

BENEDICK.

To bind me, or undo me; one of them.

Signior Leonato, truth it is, good signior,

Your niece regards me with an eye of favour.

LEONATO.

That eye my daughter lent her. 'Tis most true.

BENEDICK.

And I do with an eye of love requite her.

LEONATO.

The sight whereof I think, you had from me,

From Claudio, and the Prince. But what's your will?

BENEDICK.

Your answer, sir, is enigmatical:

But, for my will, my will is your good will

May stand with ours, this day to be conjoin'd

In the state of honourable marriage:

In which, good friar, I shall desire your help.

LEONATO.

My heart is with your liking.

FRIAR.

And my help. Here comes the Prince and Claudio.

Enter Don Pedro and Claudio, with Attendants.

DON PEDRO.

Good morrow to this fair assembly.

LEONATO.

Good morrow, Prince; good morrow, Claudio:

We here attend you. Are you yet determin'd

Today to marry with my brother's daughter?

CLAUDIO.

I'll hold my mind, were she an Ethiope.

LEONATO.

Call her forth, brother: here's the friar ready.

[Exit Antonio.]

DON PEDRO.

Good morrow, Benedick. Why, what's the matter,

That you have such a February face,

So full of frost, of storm and cloudiness?

CLAUDIO.

I think he thinks upon the savage bull.

Tush! fear not, man, we'll tip thy horns with gold,

And all Europa shall rejoice at thee,

As once Europa did at lusty Jove,

When he would play the noble beast in love.

BENEDICK.

Bull Jove, sir, had an amiable low:

And some such strange bull leap'd your father's cow,

And got a calf in that same noble feat,

Much like to you, for you have just his bleat.

CLAUDIO.

For this I owe you: here comes other reckonings.

Re-enter Antonio, with the ladies masked.

Which is the lady I must seize upon?

ANTONIO.

This same is she, and I do give you her.

CLAUDIO.

Why then, she's mine. Sweet, let me see your face.

LEONATO.

No, that you shall not, till you take her hand

Before this friar, and swear to marry her.

CLAUDIO.

Give me your hand: before this holy friar,

I am your husband, if you like of me.

HERO.

And when I liv'd, I was your other wife:

[Unmasking.] And when you lov'd, you were my other husband.

CLAUDIO.

Another Hero!

HERO.

Nothing certainer:

One Hero died defil'd, but I do live,

And surely as I live, I am a maid.

DON PEDRO.

The former Hero! Hero that is dead!

LEONATO.

She died, my lord, but whiles her slander liv'd.

FRIAR.

All this amazement can I qualify:

When after that the holy rites are ended,

I'll tell you largely of fair Hero's death:

Meantime, let wonder seem familiar,

And to the chapel let us presently.

BENEDICK.

Soft and fair, friar. Which is Beatrice?

BEATRICE.

[Unmasking.] I answer to that name. What is your will?

BENEDICK.

Do not you love me?

BEATRICE.

Why, no; no more than reason.

BENEDICK.

Why, then, your uncle and the Prince and Claudio

Have been deceived; for they swore you did.

BEATRICE.

Do not you love me?

BENEDICK.

Troth, no; no more than reason.

BEATRICE.

Why, then my cousin, Margaret, and Ursula,

Are much deceiv'd; for they did swear you did.

BENEDICK.

They swore that you were almost sick for me.

BEATRICE.

They swore that you were well-nigh dead for me.

BENEDICK.

'Tis no such matter. Then you do not love me?

BEATRICE.

No, truly, but in friendly recompense.

LEONATO.

Come, cousin, I am sure you love the gentleman.

CLAUDIO.

And I'll be sworn upon 't that he loves her;

For here's a paper written in his hand,

A halting sonnet of his own pure brain,

Fashion'd to Beatrice.

HERO.

And here's another,

Writ in my cousin's hand, stolen from her pocket,

Containing her affection unto Benedick.

BENEDICK.

A miracle! here's our own hands against our hearts. Come, I will have thee; but, by this light, I take thee for pity.

BEATRICE.

I would not deny you; but, by this good day, I yield upon great persuasion, and partly to save your life, for I was told you were in a consumption.

BENEDICK.

Peace! I will stop your mouth. [Kisses her.]

DON PEDRO.

How dost thou, Benedick, the married man?

BENEDICK.

I'll tell thee what, Prince; a college of witcrackers cannout flout me out of my humour. Dost thou think I care for a satire or an epigram? No; if man will be beaten with brains, a' shall wear nothing handsome about him. In brief, since I do purpose to marry, I will think nothing to any purpose that the world can say against it; and therefore never flout at me for what I have said against it, for man is a giddy thing, and this is my conclusion. For thy part, Claudio, I did think to have beaten thee; but, in that thou art like to be my kinsman, live unbruised, and love my cousin.

CLAUDIO.

I had well hoped thou wouldst have denied Beatrice, that I might have cudgelled thee out of thy single life, to make thee a double-dealer; which, out of question, thou wilt be, if my cousin do not look exceeding narrowly to thee.

BENEDICK.

Come, come, we are friends. Let's have a dance ere we are married, that we may lighten our own hearts and our wives' heels.

LEONATO.

We'll have dancing afterward.

BENEDICK.

First, of my word; therefore play, music! Prince, thou art sad; get thee a wife, get thee a wife: there is no staff more reverent than one tipped with horn.

Enter Messenger.

MESSENGER.

My lord, your brother John is ta'en in flight,

And brought with armed men back to Messina.

BENEDICK.

Think not on him till tomorrow: I'll devise thee brave punishments for him. Strike up, pipers!

[Dance. Exeunt.]

About Author

Shakespeare produced most of his known works between 1589 and 1613. His early plays were primarily comedies and histories and are regarded as some of the best work produced in these genres. Until about 1608, he wrote mainly tragedies, among them Hamlet, Othello, King Lear, and Macbeth, all considered to be among the finest works in the English language. In the last phase of his life, he wrote tragicomedies (also known as romances) and collaborated with other playwrights.

Many of Shakespeare's plays were published in editions of varying quality and accuracy in his lifetime. However, in 1623, two fellow actors and friends of Shakespeare's, John Heminges and Henry Condell, published a more definitive text known as the First Folio, a posthumous collected edition of Shakespeare's dramatic works that included all but two of his plays. The volume was prefaced with a poem by Ben Jonson, in which Jonson presciently hails Shakespeare in a now-famous quote as "not of an age, but for all time".

Throughout the 20th and 21st centuries, Shakespeare's works have been continually adapted and rediscovered by new movements in scholarship and performance. His plays remain popular and are studied, performed, and reinterpreted through various cultural and political contexts around the world.

Early life

William Shakespeare was the son of John Shakespeare, an alderman and a successful glover (glove-maker) originally from Snitterfield, and Mary Arden, the daughter of an affluent landowning farmer. He was born in Stratford-upon-Avon and baptised there on 26 April 1564. His actual date of birth remains unknown, but is traditionally observed on 23 April, Saint George's Day. This date, which can be traced to a mistake made by an 18th-century scholar, has proved appealing to biographers because Shakespeare died on the same date in 1616. He was the third of eight children, and the eldest surviving son.

Although no attendance records for the period survive, most biographers agree that Shakespeare was probably educated at the King's New School in Stratford, a free school chartered in 1553, about a quarter-mile (400 m) from his home. Grammar schools varied in quality during the Elizabethan era, but grammar school curricula were largely similar: the basic Latin text was standardised by royal decree, and the school would have provided an intensive education in grammar based upon Latin classical authors.

At the age of 18, Shakespeare married 26-year-old Anne Hathaway. The consistory court of the Diocese of Worcester issued a marriage licence on 27 November 1582. The next day, two of Hathaway's neighbours posted bonds guaranteeing that no lawful claims impeded the marriage. The ceremony may have been arranged in some haste since the Worcester chancellor allowed the marriage banns to be read once instead of the usual three times, and six months after the marriage Anne gave birth to a daughter, Susanna, baptised 26 May 1583. Twins, son Hamnet and daughter Judith, followed almost two years later and were baptised 2 February 1585. Hamnet died of unknown causes at the age of 11 and was buried 11 August 1596.

After the birth of the twins, Shakespeare left few historical traces until he is mentioned as part of the London theatre scene in 1592. The exception is the appearance of his name in the "complaints bill" of a law case before the Queen's Bench court at Westminster dated Michaelmas Term 1588 and 9 October 1589. Scholars refer to the years between 1585 and 1592 as Shakespeare's "lost years". Biographers attempting to account for this period have reported many apocryphal stories. Nicholas Rowe, Shakespeare's first biographer, recounted a Stratford legend that Shakespeare fled the town for London to escape prosecution for deer poaching in the estate of local squire Thomas Lucy. Shakespeare is also supposed to have taken his revenge on Lucy by writing a scurrilous ballad about him. Another 18th-century story has Shakespeare starting his theatrical career minding the horses of theatre patrons in London. John Aubrey reported that Shakespeare had been a country schoolmaster. Some 20th-century scholars have suggested that Shakespeare may have been employed as a schoolmaster by Alexander

Hoghton of Lancashire, a Catholic landowner who named a certain "William Shakeshafte" in his will. Little evidence substantiates such stories other than hearsay collected after his death, and Shakeshafte was a common name in the Lancashire area.

London and theatrical career

It is not known definitively when Shakespeare began writing, but contemporary allusions and records of performances show that several of his plays were on the London stage by 1592. By then, he was sufficiently known in London to be attacked in print by the playwright Robert Greene in his Groats-Worth of Wit:

... there is an upstart Crow, beautified with our feathers, that with his Tiger's heart wrapped in a Player's hide, supposes he is as well able to bombast out a blank verse as the best of you: and being an absolute Johannes factotum, is in his own conceit the only Shake-scene in a country.

Scholars differ on the exact meaning of Greene's words, but most agree that Greene was accusing Shakespeare of reaching above his rank in trying to match such university-educated writers as Christopher Marlowe, Thomas Nashe, and Greene himself (the so-called "University Wits"). The italicised phrase parodying the line "Oh, tiger's heart wrapped in a woman's hide" from Shakespeare's Henry VI, Part 3, along with the pun "Shake-scene", clearly identify Shakespeare as Greene's target. As used here, Johannes Factotum ("Jack of all trades") refers to a second-rate tinkerer with the work of others, rather than the more common "universal genius".

Greene's attack is the earliest surviving mention of Shakespeare's work in the theatre. Biographers suggest that his career may have begun any time from the mid-1580s to just before Greene's remarks. After 1594, Shakespeare's plays were performed only by the Lord Chamberlain's Men, a company owned by a group of players, including Shakespeare, that soon became the leading playing company in London. After the death of Queen Elizabeth in 1603, the company was awarded a royal patent by the new King James I, and changed its name to the King's Men.

"All the world's a stage,

and all the men and women merely players:

they have their exits and their entrances;

and one man in his time plays many parts ..."

—As You Like It, Act II, Scene 7, 139–142

In 1599, a partnership of members of the company built their own theatre on the south bank of the River Thames, which they named the Globe. In 1608, the partnership also took over the Blackfriars indoor theatre. Extant records of Shakespeare's property purchases and investments indicate that his association with the company made him a wealthy man, and in 1597, he bought the second-largest house in Stratford, New Place, and in 1605, invested in a share of the parish tithes in Stratford.

Some of Shakespeare's plays were published in quarto editions, beginning in 1594, and by 1598, his name had become a selling point and began to appear on the title pages. Shakespeare continued to act in his own and other plays after his success as a playwright. The 1616 edition of Ben Jonson's Works names him on the cast lists for Every Man in His Humour (1598) and Sejanus His Fall (1603). The absence of his name from the 1605 cast list for Jonson's Volpone is taken by some scholars as a sign that his acting career was nearing its end. The First Folio of 1623, however, lists Shakespeare as one of "the Principal Actors in all these Plays", some of which were first staged after Volpone, although we cannot know for certain which roles he played. In 1610, John Davies of Hereford wrote that "good Will" played "kingly" roles. In 1709, Rowe passed down a tradition that Shakespeare played the ghost of Hamlet's father. Later traditions maintain that he also played Adam in As You Like It, and the Chorus in Henry V, though scholars doubt the sources of that information.

Throughout his career, Shakespeare divided his time between London and Stratford. In 1596, the year before he bought New Place as his family home in Stratford, Shakespeare was living in the parish of St. Helen's, Bishopsgate, north of the River Thames. He moved across the river to Southwark by 1599, the same year his company constructed the Globe Theatre there. By 1604, he had moved north of the river again, to an area north of St Paul's Cathedral with many fine houses. There, he rented rooms from a French Huguenot named Christopher Mountjoy, a maker of ladies' wigs and other headgear.

Later years and death

Rowe was the first biographer to record the tradition, repeated by Johnson, that Shakespeare retired to Stratford "some years before his death". He was still working as an actor in London in 1608; in an answer to the sharers' petition in 1635, Cuthbert Burbage stated that after purchasing the lease of the Blackfriars Theatre in 1608 from Henry Evans, the King's Men "placed men players" there, "which were Heminges, Condell, Shakespeare, etc.". However, it is perhaps relevant that the bubonic plague raged in London throughout 1609. The London public playhouses were repeatedly closed during extended outbreaks of the plague (a total of over 60 months closure between May 1603 and February 1610), which meant there was often no acting work. Retirement from all work was uncommon at that time. Shakespeare continued to visit London during the years 1611–1614. In 1612, he was called as a witness in Bellott v. Mountjoy, a court case concerning the marriage settlement of Mountjoy's daughter, Mary. In March 1613, he bought a gatehouse in the former Blackfriars priory; and from November 1614, he was in London for several weeks with his son-in-law, John Hall. After 1610, Shakespeare wrote fewer plays, and none are attributed to him after 1613. His last three plays were collaborations, probably with John Fletcher, who succeeded him as the house playwright of the King's Men.

Shakespeare died on 23 April 1616, at the age of 52. He died within a month of signing his will, a document which he begins by describing himself as being in "perfect health". No extant contemporary source explains how or why he died. Half a century later, John Ward, the vicar of Stratford, wrote in his notebook: "Shakespeare, Drayton, and Ben Jonson had a merry meeting and, it seems, drank too hard, for Shakespeare died of a fever there contracted", not an impossible scenario since Shakespeare knew Jonson and Drayton. Of the tributes from fellow authors, one refers to his relatively sudden death: "We wondered, Shakespeare, that thou went'st so soon / From the world's stage to the grave's tiring room."

He was survived by his wife and two daughters. Susanna had married a physician, John Hall, in 1607, and Judith had married Thomas Quiney, a vintner, two months before Shakespeare's death. Shakespeare signed his last will and testament on 25 March 1616; the following day, his new son-in-law, Thomas Quiney was found guilty of fathering an illegitimate son by Margaret Wheeler, who had died during childbirth. Thomas was ordered by the church court to do public penance, which would have caused much shame and embarrassment for the Shakespeare family.

Shakespeare bequeathed the bulk of his large estate to his elder daughter Susanna under stipulations that she pass it down intact to "the first son of her body". The Quineys had three children, all of whom died without marrying. The Halls had one child, Elizabeth, who married twice but died without children in 1670, ending Shakespeare's direct line. Shakespeare's will scarcely mentions his wife, Anne, who was probably entitled to one-third of his estate automatically. He did make a point, however, of leaving her "my second best bed", a bequest that has led to much speculation. Some scholars see the bequest as an insult to Anne, whereas others believe that the second-best bed would have been the matrimonial bed and therefore rich in significance.

Shakespeare was buried in the chancel of the Holy Trinity Church two days after his death. The epitaph carved into the stone slab covering his grave includes a curse against moving his bones, which was carefully avoided during restoration of the church in 2008:

Good frend for Iesvs sake forbeare,

To digg the dvst encloased heare.

Bleste be Middle English the.svg man Middle English that.svg spares thes stones,

And cvrst be he Middle English that.svg moves my bones.

(Modern spelling: Good friend, for Jesus' sake forbear, / To dig the dust enclosed here. / Blessed be the man that spares these stones, / And cursed be he that moves my bones.)

Some time before 1623, a funerary monument was erected in his memory on the north wall, with a half-effigy of him in the act of writing. Its plaque compares him to Nestor, Socrates, and Virgil. In 1623, in conjunction with the publication of the First Folio, the Droeshout engraving was published.

Shakespeare has been commemorated in many statues and memorials around the world, including funeral monuments in Southwark Cathedral and Poets' Corner in Westminster Abbey.

Plays

Most playwrights of the period typically collaborated with others at some point, and critics agree that Shakespeare did the same, mostly early and late in his career. Some attributions, such as Titus Andronicus and the early history plays, remain controversial while The Two Noble Kinsmen and the lost Cardenio have well-attested contemporary documentation. Textual evidence also supports the view that several of the plays were revised by other writers after their original composition.

The first recorded works of Shakespeare are Richard III and the three parts of Henry VI, written in the early 1590s during a vogue for historical drama. Shakespeare's plays are difficult to date precisely, however, and studies of the texts suggest that Titus Andronicus, The Comedy of Errors, The Taming of the Shrew, and The Two Gentlemen of Verona may also belong to Shakespeare's earliest period. His first histories, which draw heavily on the 1587 edition of Raphael Holinshed's Chronicles of England, Scotland, and Ireland, dramatise the destructive results of weak or corrupt rule and have been interpreted as a justification for the origins of the Tudor dynasty. The early plays were influenced by the works of other Elizabethan dramatists, especially Thomas Kyd and Christopher Marlowe, by the traditions of medieval drama, and by the plays of Seneca. The Comedy of Errors was also based on classical models, but no source for The Taming of the Shrew has been found, though it is related to a separate play of the same name and may have derived from a folk story. Like The Two Gentlemen of Verona, in which two friends appear to approve of rape, the Shrew's story of the taming of a woman's independent spirit by a man sometimes troubles modern critics, directors, and audiences.

Shakespeare's early classical and Italianate comedies, containing tight double plots and precise comic sequences, give way in the mid-1590s to the romantic atmosphere of his most acclaimed comedies. A Midsummer Night's Dream is a witty mixture of romance, fairy magic, and comic lowlife scenes. Shakespeare's next comedy, the equally romantic Merchant of Venice, contains a portrayal of the vengeful Jewish moneylender Shylock, which reflects Elizabethan views but may appear derogatory to modern audiences. The wit and wordplay of Much Ado About Nothing, the charming rural setting of As You Like It, and the lively merrymaking of Twelfth Night complete Shakespeare's sequence of great comedies. After the lyrical Richard II, written almost entirely in verse, Shakespeare introduced prose comedy into the histories of the late 1590s, Henry IV, parts 1 and 2, and Henry V. His characters become more complex and tender as he switches deftly between comic and serious scenes, prose and poetry, and achieves the narrative variety of his mature work. This period begins and ends with two tragedies: Romeo and Juliet, the famous romantic tragedy of sexually charged adolescence, love, and death; and Julius Caesar—based on Sir Thomas North's 1579 translation of Plutarch's Parallel Lives—which introduced a new kind of drama. According to Shakespearean scholar James Shapiro, in Julius Caesar, "the various strands of politics, character, inwardness, contemporary events, even Shakespeare's own reflections on the act of writing, began to infuse each other".

In the early 17th century, Shakespeare wrote the so-called "problem plays" Measure for Measure, Troilus and Cressida, and All's Well That Ends Well and a number of his best known tragedies. Many critics believe that Shakespeare's greatest tragedies represent the peak of his art. The titular hero of one of Shakespeare's greatest tragedies, Hamlet, has probably been discussed more than any other Shakespearean character, especially for his famous soliloquy which begins "To be or not to be; that is the question". Unlike the introverted Hamlet, whose fatal flaw is hesitation, the heroes of the tragedies that followed, Othello and King Lear, are undone by hasty errors of judgement. The plots of Shakespeare's tragedies often hinge on such fatal errors or flaws, which overturn order and destroy the hero and those

274

he loves. In Othello, the villain Iago stokes Othello's sexual jealousy to the point where he murders the innocent wife who loves him. In King Lear, the old king commits the tragic error of giving up his powers, initiating the events which lead to the torture and blinding of the Earl of Gloucester and the murder of Lear's youngest daughter Cordelia. According to the critic Frank Kermode, "the play-offers neither its good characters nor its audience any relief from its cruelty". In Macbeth, the shortest and most compressed of Shakespeare's tragedies, uncontrollable ambition incites Macbeth and his wife, Lady Macbeth, to murder the rightful king and usurp the throne until their own guilt destroys them in turn. In this play, Shakespeare adds a supernatural element to the tragic structure. His last major tragedies, Antony and Cleopatra and Coriolanus, contain some of Shakespeare's finest poetry and were considered his most successful tragedies by the poet and critic T.S. Eliot.

In his final period, Shakespeare turned to romance or tragicomedy and completed three more major plays: Cymbeline, The Winter's Tale, and The Tempest, as well as the collaboration, Pericles, Prince of Tyre. Less bleak than the tragedies, these four plays are graver in tone than the comedies of the 1590s, but they end with reconciliation and the forgiveness of potentially tragic errors. Some commentators have seen this change in mood as evidence of a more serene view of life on Shakespeare's part, but it may merely reflect the theatrical fashion of the day. Shakespeare collaborated on two further surviving plays, Henry VIII and The Two Noble Kinsmen, probably with John Fletcher.

Performances

It is not clear for which companies Shakespeare wrote his early plays. The title page of the 1594 edition of Titus Andronicus reveals that the play had been acted by three different troupes. After the plagues of 1592–3, Shakespeare's plays were performed by his own company at The Theatre and the Curtain in Shoreditch, north of the Thames. Londoners flocked there to see the first part of Henry IV, Leonard Digges recording, "Let but Falstaff come, Hal, Poins, the rest ... and you scarce shall have a room". When the company found themselves in dispute with their landlord, they pulled The

Theatre down and used the timbers to construct the Globe Theatre, the first playhouse built by actors for actors, on the south bank of the Thames at Southwark. The Globe opened in autumn 1599, with Julius Caesar one of the first plays staged. Most of Shakespeare's greatest post-1599 plays were written for the Globe, including Hamlet, Othello, and King Lear.

After the Lord Chamberlain's Men were renamed the King's Men in 1603, they entered a special relationship with the new King James. Although the performance records are patchy, the King's Men performed seven of Shakespeare's plays at court between 1 November 1604, and 31 October 1605, including two performances of The Merchant of Venice. After 1608, they performed at the indoor Blackfriars Theatre during the winter and the Globe during the summer. The indoor setting, combined with the Jacobean fashion for lavishly staged masques, allowed Shakespeare to introduce more elaborate stage devices. In Cymbeline, for example, Jupiter descends "in thunder and lightning, sitting upon an eagle: he throws a thunderbolt. The ghosts fall on their knees."

The actors in Shakespeare's company included the famous Richard Burbage, William Kempe, Henry Condell and John Heminges. Burbage played the leading role in the first performances of many of Shakespeare's plays, including Richard III, Hamlet, Othello, and King Lear. The popular comic actor Will Kempe played the servant Peter in Romeo and Juliet and Dogberry in Much Ado About Nothing, among other characters. He was replaced around 1600 by Robert Armin, who played roles such as Touchstone in As You Like It and the fool in King Lear. In 1613, Sir Henry Wotton recorded that Henry VIII "was set forth with many extraordinary circumstances of pomp and ceremony". On 29 June, however, a cannon set fire to the thatch of the Globe and burned the theatre to the ground, an event which pinpoints the date of a Shakespeare play with rare precision.

Textual sources

In 1623, John Heminges and Henry Condell, two of Shakespeare's friends from the King's Men, published the First Folio, a collected edition of Shakespeare's plays. It contained 36 texts, including 18 printed for the first time. Many of the plays had already appeared in quarto versions—flimsy books made from sheets of paper folded twice to make four leaves. No evidence suggests that Shakespeare approved these editions, which the First Folio describes as "stol'n and surreptitious copies". Nor did Shakespeare plan or expect his works to survive in any form at all; those works likely would have faded into oblivion but for his friends' spontaneous idea, after his death, to create and publish the First Folio.

Alfred Pollard termed some of the pre-1623 versions as "bad quartos" because of their adapted, paraphrased or garbled texts, which may in places have been reconstructed from memory. Where several versions of a play survive, each differs from the other. The differences may stem from copying or printing errors, from notes by actors or audience members, or from Shakespeare's own papers. In some cases, for example, Hamlet, Troilus and Cressida, and Othello, Shakespeare could have revised the texts between the quarto and folio editions. In the case of King Lear, however, while most modern editions do conflate them, the 1623 folio version is so different from the 1608 quarto that the Oxford Shakespeare prints them both, arguing that they cannot be conflated without confusion.

Influence from neighbours in London

Ten years of research by Geoffrey Marsh (museum director) of the Victoria and Albert Museum in London may have shown that Shakespeare got many of the ideas and information for his plays, from his neighbours that he lived near in London in the late 1590s.

Geoffrey Marsh found the site of Shakespeare's house in St Helen's Church, Bishopsgate parish, at the corner of St.Helen's churchyard and Bishopsgate Street, north of the churchyard, from the records of the Leathersellers Company. Many wealthy and notable people (including Sir John Spencer and Dr. Edward Jorden and Dr. Peter Turner), with connections across Europe, lived near Shakespeare.

Poems

In 1593 and 1594, when the theatres were closed because of plague,

Shakespeare published two narrative poems on sexual themes, Venus and Adonis and The Rape of Lucrece. He dedicated them to Henry Wriothesley, Earl of Southampton. In Venus and Adonis, an innocent Adonis rejects the sexual advances of Venus; while in The Rape of Lucrece, the virtuous wife Lucrece is raped by the lustful Tarquin. Influenced by Ovid's Metamorphoses, the poems show the guilt and moral confusion that result from uncontrolled lust. Both proved popular and were often reprinted during Shakespeare's lifetime. A third narrative poem, A Lover's Complaint, in which a young woman laments her seduction by a persuasive suitor, was printed in the first edition of the Sonnets in 1609. Most scholars now accept that Shakespeare wrote A Lover's Complaint. Critics consider that its fine qualities are marred by leaden effects. The Phoenix and the Turtle, printed in Robert Chester's 1601 Love's Martyr, mourns the deaths of the legendary phoenix and his lover, the faithful turtle dove. In 1599, two early drafts of sonnets 138 and 144 appeared in The Passionate Pilgrim, published under Shakespeare's name but without his permission.

Sonnets

Published in 1609, the Sonnets were the last of Shakespeare's non-dramatic works to be printed. Scholars are not certain when each of the 154 sonnets was composed, but evidence suggests that Shakespeare wrote sonnets throughout his career for a private readership. Even before the two unauthorised sonnets appeared in The Passionate Pilgrim in 1599, Francis Meres had referred in 1598 to Shakespeare's "sugred Sonnets among his private friends". Few analysts believe that the published collection follows Shakespeare's intended sequence. He seems to have planned two contrasting series: one about uncontrollable lust for a married woman of dark complexion (the "dark lady"), and one about conflicted love for a fair young man (the "fair youth"). It remains unclear if these figures represent real individuals, or if the authorial "I" who addresses them represents Shakespeare himself, though Wordsworth believed that with the sonnets "Shakespeare unlocked his heart".

"Shall I compare thee to a summer's day?

Thou art more lovely and more temperate ..."

278

—Lines from Shakespeare's Sonnet 18.

The 1609 edition was dedicated to a "Mr. W.H.", credited as "the only begetter" of the poems. It is not known whether this was written by Shakespeare himself or by the publisher, Thomas Thorpe, whose initials appear at the foot of the dedication page; nor is it known who Mr. W.H. was, despite numerous theories, or whether Shakespeare even authorised the publication. Critics praise the Sonnets as a profound meditation on the nature of love, sexual passion, procreation, death, and time.

Style

Shakespeare's first plays were written in the conventional style of the day. He wrote them in a stylised language that does not always spring naturally from the needs of the characters or the drama. The poetry depends on extended, sometimes elaborate metaphors and conceits, and the language is often rhetorical—written for actors to declaim rather than speak. The grand speeches in Titus Andronicus, in the view of some critics, often hold up the action, for example; and the verse in The Two Gentlemen of Verona has been described as stilted.

However, Shakespeare soon began to adapt the traditional styles to his own purposes. The opening soliloquy of Richard III has its roots in the self-declaration of Vice in medieval drama. At the same time, Richard's vivid self-awareness looks forward to the soliloquies of Shakespeare's mature plays. No single play marks a change from the traditional to the freer style. Shakespeare combined the two throughout his career, with Romeo and Juliet perhaps the best example of the mixing of the styles. By the time of Romeo and Juliet, Richard II, and A Midsummer Night's Dream in the mid-1590s, Shakespeare had begun to write a more natural poetry. He increasingly tuned his metaphors and images to the needs of the drama itself.

Shakespeare's standard poetic form was blank verse, composed in iambic pentameter. In practice, this meant that his verse was usually unrhymed and consisted of ten syllables to a line, spoken with a stress on every second syllable. The blank verse of his early plays is quite different from that of his later ones. It is often beautiful, but its sentences tend to start, pause, and finish at the end of lines, with the risk of monotony. Once Shakespeare mastered traditional blank verse, he began to interrupt and vary its flow. This technique releases the new power and flexibility of the poetry in plays such as Julius Caesar and Hamlet. Shakespeare uses it, for example, to convey the turmoil in Hamlet's mind:

> Sir, in my heart there was a kind of fighting
>
> That would not let me sleep. Methought I lay
>
> Worse than the mutines in the bilboes. Rashly—
>
> And prais'd be rashness for it—let us know
>
> Our indiscretion sometimes serves us well ...
>
> —Hamlet, Act 5, Scene 2, 4–8

After Hamlet, Shakespeare varied his poetic style further, particularly in the more emotional passages of the late tragedies. The literary critic A. C. Bradley described this style as "more concentrated, rapid, varied, and, in construction, less regular, not seldom twisted or elliptical". In the last phase of his career, Shakespeare adopted many techniques to achieve these effects. These included run-on lines, irregular pauses and stops, and extreme variations in sentence structure and length. In Macbeth, for example, the language darts from one unrelated metaphor or simile to another: "was the hope drunk/ Wherein you dressed yourself?" (1.7.35–38); "... pity, like a naked new-born babe/ Striding the blast, or heaven's cherubim, hors'd/ Upon the sightless couriers of the air ..." (1.7.21–25). The listener is challenged to complete the sense. The late romances, with their shifts in time and surprising turns of plot, inspired a last poetic style in which long and short sentences are set against one another, clauses are piled up, subject and object are reversed, and words are omitted, creating an effect of spontaneity.

Shakespeare combined poetic genius with a practical sense of the theatre. Like all playwrights of the time, he dramatised stories from sources such as Plutarch and Holinshed. He reshaped each plot to create several centres of interest and to show as many sides of a narrative to the audience as

280

possible. This strength of design ensures that a Shakespeare play can survive translation, cutting and wide interpretation without loss to its core drama. As Shakespeare's mastery grew, he gave his characters clearer and more varied motivations and distinctive patterns of speech. He preserved aspects of his earlier style in the later plays, however. In Shakespeare's late romances, he deliberately returned to a more artificial style, which emphasised the illusion of theatre.

Influence

Shakespeare's work has made a lasting impression on later theatre and literature. In particular, he expanded the dramatic potential of characterisation, plot, language, and genre. Until Romeo and Juliet, for example, romance had not been viewed as a worthy topic for tragedy. Soliloquies had been used mainly to convey information about characters or events, but Shakespeare used them to explore characters' minds. His work heavily influenced later poetry. The Romantic poets attempted to revive Shakespearean verse drama, though with little success. Critic George Steiner described all English verse dramas from Coleridge to Tennyson as "feeble variations on Shakespearean themes."

Shakespeare influenced novelists such as Thomas Hardy, William Faulkner, and Charles Dickens. The American novelist Herman Melville's soliloquies owe much to Shakespeare; his Captain Ahab in Moby-Dick is a classic tragic hero, inspired by King Lear. Scholars have identified 20,000 pieces of music linked to Shakespeare's works. These include three operas by Giuseppe Verdi, Macbeth, Otello and Falstaff, whose critical standing compares with that of the source plays. Shakespeare has also inspired many painters, including the Romantics and the Pre-Raphaelites. The Swiss Romantic artist Henry Fuseli, a friend of William Blake, even translated Macbeth into German. The psychoanalyst Sigmund Freud drew on Shakespearean psychology, in particular, that of Hamlet, for his theories of human nature.

In Shakespeare's day, English grammar, spelling, and pronunciation were less standardised than they are now, and his use of language helped shape modern English. Samuel Johnson quoted him more often than any other author in his A Dictionary of the English Language, the first serious work of its type. Expressions such as "with bated breath" (Merchant of Venice) and "a foregone conclusion" (Othello) have found their way into everyday English speech.

Works

Classification of the plays

Shakespeare's works include the 36 plays printed in the First Folio of 1623, listed according to their folio classification as comedies, histories, and tragedies. Two plays not included in the First Folio, The Two Noble Kinsmen and Pericles, Prince of Tyre, are now accepted as part of the canon, with today's scholars agreeing that Shakespeare made major contributions to the writing of both. No Shakespearean poems were included in the First Folio.

In the late 19th century, Edward Dowden classified four of the late comedies as romances, and though many scholars prefer to call them tragicomedies, Dowden's term is often used. In 1896, Frederick S. Boas coined the term "problem plays" to describe four plays: All's Well That Ends Well, Measure for Measure, Troilus and Cressida, and Hamlet. "Dramas as singular in theme and temper cannot be strictly called comedies or tragedies", he wrote. "We may, therefore, borrow a convenient phrase from the theatre of today and class them together as Shakespeare's problem plays." The term, much debated and sometimes applied to other plays, remains in use, though Hamlet is definitively classed as a tragedy. (Source: Wikipedia)

CPSIA information can be obtained
at www.ICGtesting.com
Printed in the USA
BVHW030933120919
558270BV00007B/139/P

9 789353 835309